Walter Gerald Cooper

The Piedmont Region

Embracing Georgia, Alabama, Florida and the Carolinas

Walter Gerald Cooper

The Piedmont Region
Embracing Georgia, Alabama, Florida and the Carolinas

ISBN/EAN: 9783337111083

Printed in Europe, USA, Canada, Australia, Japan

Cover: Foto ©ninafisch / pixelio.de

More available books at **www.hansebooks.com**

THE
Piedmont Region

EMBRACING

GEORGIA, ALABAMA, FLORIDA
AND THE CAROLINAS.

PUBLISHED BY THE

Southern Immigration and Improvement Co.

45 NORTH BROAD ST., ATLANTA, GA.

EDITED BY
W. G. COOPER.
CHIEF DEPARTMENT PUBLICITY AND PROMOTION COTTON STATES
AND INTERNATIONAL EXPOSITION.

ATLANTA, GA.:
CHAS. P. BYRD, PUBLISHER AND PRINTER.
1895.

PUBLISHERS NOTICE.

The Southern Immigration and Improvement Company publishes this book for the purpose of letting the world know what the Piedmont region has to offer farmers, fruit-growers, truck-gardeners, stock-raisers, miners, manufacturers and capitalists. The facts have been obtained from reliable sources and may be relied on as absolutely correct. We have placed no advertisements in this volume. It contains unbiased information, and was prepared without reference to the individual interests of clients, the object being to put before the public something upon which it could rely with the utmost confidence. Those who wish to pursue their inquiries further will be supplied with another volume which gives details of property offered for sale within the territory treated of in the following pages.

SOUTHERN IMMIGRATION AND IMPROVEMENT CO.

JAMES P. DAY,
President.

J. MARK BISHOP,
Sec. & Treas.

J. H. MOUNTAIN,
Manager.

45 North Broad St., ATLANTA, GA.

INDEX.

Introduction,
The Soil and Its Agricultural Value.
Climate and Health..........
Agriculture
Truck Farming
Fruit Growing..
Dairying..
Transportation..
Manufactures....
Minerals of Georgia.....
Wealth, Debt and Taxation.
Education in Georgia......
Labor
Markets..
Timber
Building Stones and Timber resources.
Alabama....
Florida... ....
The Carolinas.....
Cities of the Piedmont region.....
The Cotton States and International Exposition..

PREFACE.

It was not attempted in the few pages within these covers to treat exhaustively of the Piedmont region. Volumes have been written on different branches of the subject, and it is only possible to give in outline the salient features; but it was intended to do the work thoroughly and accurately as far as it went, so that a reader unfamiliar with the subject would not be led astray. Upon the degree of success with which the task has been accomplished depends the usefulness of this little volume.

In this connection I wish to make due acknowledgment for aid which I have received from Dr. H. C. White, Prof. C. M. Strahn, Prof. N. P. Pratt, Ex-State School Commissioner S. D. Bradwell, Mr. G. H. Miller and Col. R. J. Redding, who wrote the chapters on Soils, Building Material, Minerals, Education, Fruit Growing, and Dairying; also to State Treasurer R. U. Hardeman, for information concerning State finances, and to State Commissioner R. T. Nesbitt, for information on agriculture. W. G. COOPER.

Introduction.

Georgia, Alabama, the Carolinas and East Tennessee constitute the Piedmont region of North America. Here the lower end of the Appalachian chain spreads out like a gigantic cornucopia, pouring its wealth upon the plain; here the Atlantic ocean reaches far inward to catch its freight of nature's rich profusion, and floats the largest ships nearer to the Western granary than at any other part of the long coast; here the gulf approaches with moist south winds that soothe and fructify the earth; and here the primeval forest, wrapping the folds of the great cornucopia in its evergreen mantle, sweeps from Hatteras to the Mexican border. Descending by easy stages from mountain to plain, this marvelous region presents in quick succession almost the entire vegetable series of the United States. This is the hospitable home of the husbandman, the vine dresser, the fruit grower and the florist. Here, too, is nature's ideal seat of industry, with materials spread out in endless profusion, and the bracing breezes of the hill country pouring out an ærial champagne that stirs men to effort. This incomparable tonic of ozone gives to the people of the Piedmont region that transcendent energy by which, as in Atlanta, they rise superior to obstacles, and build even upon occasional failure the fabric of success.

Georgia is the first State of the South in point of progress. In the combined products of agriculture and industry she has outstripped her neighbors. She was the first to recover from the devastation of the war, and Atlanta, the city which was left in ashes by Sherman's army, bids fair to become the Southern metropolis.

In the readjustment of agriculture made necessary by the abolition of slavery, Georgia has taken the lead. Plantations have been divided and subdivided, and intensive farming becomes more and more popular. Forms of agriculture which were mere incidents of household economy have become staple crops. Before the war the watermelon was the planter's perquisite—one of the luxuries of rural life. Now it is the great summer crop of southern Georgia, requiring ten thousand cars to move it and bringing large revenues to the railroads as well as to the farmer. The Georgia peach has become a staple, excelling all others in flavor, and bringing in the New York markets a higher price than the peaches of Jersey or California. Grapes flourish on the old red hills and their vintage rivals the vintage of France.

In the agriculture of the present, more labor is required to an acre. Better directed labor is the general demand, and to supply it, agricultural colleges are busying themselves with the problems of the soil. A State experiment station solves these problems, tries new methods by the rule of experience, and gives out its results in regular bulletins. The whole trend of our educational system is to equip labor with the weapons of science. The Technological school at Atlanta teaches boys how to make houses, roads, engines and everything that is wrought in wood, brass or iron. At a similar institution in Alabama at Auburn, the boys are making electric motors and dynamos up to fifteen horse power. The Georgia Institute of technology not long ago made the gearing for two hundred looms, now at work in a cotton factory in the suburbs of Atlanta. The idea of Georgia and her sister States with regard to labor is to dignify and strengthen it by equipping it with the most consummate skill that the arts can supply, and by endowing it with a knowledge of the latest contributions of science to human progress. By these means the waste places are being redeemed, and even the pine barrens are being made to bloom.

Great progress has been made in the past ten years in the building of public highways. Floyd county is a fine illustration. In 1881 there was not a good road about Rome. Now eight graded and macadamized turnpikes radiate from that point. Fifteen years ago there were but two or three Jersey cows in the county; now there are hundreds. With better roads have come better horses, better cattle and improved agriculture. Such has been the history of road making in Fulton, Bibb, Chatham, Richmond and other counties, whose good example is gradually influencing others.

The growth of education is one of the most gratifying features of the situation. Beginning after the war with no system of public schools, the State has gradually increased her equipment till the annual fund has reached $1,200,000.

Besides the common schools, the State appropriates money for several branch colleges of the State University, for an agricultural experiment station, for the Georgia Institute of Technology, for a similar institution for colored people, for a girls' industrial school, for teachers institutes, and for a State Normal school. The State University has a fund of about $40,000 a year from all sources and included in it is the State College of Agriculture and Mechanic Arts, which has been holding farmers' institutes in various parts of the State.

Working in connection with these institutions is the State Department of Agriculture, where every brand of fertilizers sold in the State is analyzed and graded. The maker is required to stamp its component parts on the sack, under penalty of a heavy fine. Any farmer can have his soil or fertilizer analyzed by the State chemist and get an expert opinion as to its needs and culture from the agricultural department or the experiment station.

It is inconceivable that a practical and progressive people, with such ideas and such institutions, should give themselves over to the carnival of riot and disorder which some deluded persons at a distance suppose to be the order of things in the South. Never was there a more egregious error. Never was a greater injustice done to an intelligent and patriotic people. Conservative in faith and jealous of public morals, the people of this region are less torn by sedition, communism or anarchy than those of any other section.

Crimes are committed in the South as elsewhere, and offenders pay the same penalty as elsewhere, but the percentage of crime is lower than in any other part of the Union. There are occasional mobs in Southern cities, as there have been in every Northern city, but nothing to compare with the scenes of violence in Pittsburgh in 1878, in Cincinnati in 1884 or in Chicago in 1894.

During the upheaval following the war, when the whole industrial system of the South was destroyed, when the ignorant slave confronted his master as an equal before the law, when the labor system was in chaos and had to be reorganized upon new and untried lines, there was some disorder, some friction and some blood shed. As a statesman of the time remarked, "It was impossible to inject four million savages into the body politic without making trouble." Mr. Lincoln's papers show that he never contemplated such a crisis of confusion, but intended to educate the negro up to citizenship gradually after emancipation. The disorder of that day was the incident of a revolution in the industrial system of the South. That revolution has progressed far toward completion. The agriculture of the South has been reorganized on the basis of free labor, and has gradually adjusted itself to the new economic conditions. The negro in the country is now laborer, tenant or proprietor of a small farm. In the towns or cities he is carpenter, bricklayer, drayman, or perhaps a small merchant at the corner grocery. Otherwise he is a servant. The educated ones are teachers, preachers, editors, mail carriers, railway mail clerks, and a few are lawyers or doctors.

Much has been said about the lynching of negroes for rape. This penalty follows the crime in any part of the Union. Recent instances have occurred in Pennsylvania, New York and Illinois. The instincts of men are the same on this subject, no matter what their latitude may be. Moralists and judges remonstrate and Governors threaten, but human blood boils at the sight of outraged virtue. There is no respite for the rapist on the face of this planet. All law and all morality condemn mob law, and steadily supplant it, except for the one offense of rapine. Here a profounder law of human nature asserts itself in every country. It seems to be an instinct akin to that of self-protection. Not one time in a hundred is a negro lynched for any other offense. Rarely are they lynched even for murder. Mobs and mob violence are rare in the South, much rarer than in other parts of the Union.

Southern people cherish the right of opinion and free speech, and respect that right in others. In no quarter of the earth is there more respect for difference of opinion. Only the anarchist, the criminal, the idle, the vicious, are regarded as enemies of society. Honest men are everywhere welcome without regard to previous political or religious affiliation. Men are valued for what they are. No one need imagine that because he or his father was an abolitionist he will be coldly received. Thousands of such men are prominent in business, in society and even in politics. Nothing could more signalize this truth than the fact that a Federal general is one of the chief executive officers of the Cotton

States and International Exposition, to be held in Atlanta this year.

Some of the best people of the Middle States have settled in Georgia during the past ten years, and they have not only been cordially received, but their methods or their enterprise, when superior to those of their neighbors, have been readily adopted. The Southern people are quick to appreciate intelligence, and eagerly study improved methods. Any man who contributes to the advancement of his profession or business, or to the good of society, may be sure of appreciation. It is the same whether he builds a city or makes two blades of grass grow where one grew before.

The situation of Georgia and the Piedmont States is a happy one, giving a climate without extremes of heat or cold, an atmosphere copiously fed with moisture from the gulf, and a soil adapted and hospitable to a great variety of products.

The records of the government show that the Piedmont region has lower temperatures than Ohio, Illinois, Missouri or Kansas in summer, while in winter the mercury seldom falls lower than 10 or 15 degrees above zero. There are no long snow-bound periods, when people are kept prisoners by the blizzard. Snow rarely remains on the ground more than a day or two. In summer the nights are generally cool, and with refreshing sleep the heat of a summer day is not hard to endure.

The rainfall is abundant and well distributed through the year, so that a total failure of crops is unknown. The record of the weather bureau at Atlanta shows an average of 53 inches, and this average is generally maintained throughout the Piedmont region.

Georgia is divided by nature into three distinct sections, with varying soil, due to different geological formations. Middle Georgia has a granite foundation, the oldest in the world, and upon this rocky base Atlanta is built. Only fifteen miles away Stone Mountain rears its venerable dome. For miles about its base quarrymen are engaged in getting out the granite blocks used in paving streets and building edifices in Baltimore, Cincinnati, Columbus and many other cities of the Northern and Middle States.

To the northwest of this primeval granite, the geological formation ascends with hardly a missing stratum to the coal measures in the northwestern corner of the State. The coal mines of Dade and Walker counties are among the best in the South, furnishing a high grade of bitumenous coal, with fine coking qualities. Farther west are the immense coalfields of Alabama.

The rapid succession of geological formations in northern Georgia is due to the breaking up of the Blue Ridge, which rises into peaks 5,000 feet high just after passing into the State, and before it breaks up into the rolling foothills of middle Georgia. Similar causes give character to the hill country of North Alabama and the Carolinas.

This variety of formation furnishes a long list of minerals, from gold to iron and manganese. The iron ores are of such richness and variety as to attract the attention of the metallurgists of the world, and the deposits of bauxite are said to be the finest in the United States.

To the south of middle Georgia are the broad plains of the tertiary and quarternary formations, with their rich sandy loam and immense forests of long leaf pine. In this section also there are deposits of phosphate rock, used in making fertilizers. The other ingredient, sulphuric acid, is extracted from the iron pyrites of the northern counties, so that the farmer finds ready in the mountains or on the plain the plant food most needed by the staple crops.

The soil of northern and middle Georgia is red and rich in iron, giving a fine flavor to fruits and furnishing the best basis for permanent culture. The valleys of creeks and rivers have rich alluvial deposits, which grow the finest fiber of cotton known to commerce. The timber of this hill country is mainly hard wood, furnishing material for flourishing manufactories in the principal cities.

The Soil and Its Agricultural Value in the Piedmont Region.

BY H. C. WHITE, PH. D., F. C. S., PRESIDENT OF THE STATE COLLEGE OF AGRICULTURE AND MECHANIC ARTS.

The "metamorphic" formation extends over a large part of the Piedmont region. In fact, if a line be drawn approximately straight across Georgia in a southwesterly direction from Augusta, on the Savannah river, to Columbus on the Chattahoochee, all of the state north of this line is within the "metamorphic," excepting the ten counties comprising the extreme northwestern corner. This metamorphic region is the mountainous or hilly portion of Georgia, extending into South Carolina, mountain-making and the metamorphism of rocks being due to the same general causes. The country is, therefore, broken and hilly but not truly mountainous. Ranges of mountains of considerable altitude lie to the northward. For healthfulness and comfort the climate is most excellent, and it is admirably adapted to a great variety of agricultural and horticultural products.

The rocks of the metamorphic formation vary somewhat in different localities, but they are generally hard, compact and silicious, the great bulk of the rock being granite, or nearly approaching granite in composition and character. At occasional points the rock is very like true granite, and is suitable for building and road-bed purposes. In the greater part of the metamorphic formation of this region the rock is seamed with occasional veins of gold-bearing quartz. The rich veins and deposits found in the counties to the north occur generally among the schistose and quartzose rocks and not among the granites.

Whilst the rock is comparatively uniform in general character, and is all, comparatively speaking, hard and compact, it is not uniform in hardness and compactness. As a consequence, erosion has carved the surface into numberless water-worn hills and valleys, giving it a "rolling" character. As a further consequence, the streams (of which there are a great number) have uneven and somewhat precipitous channels, and move with rapidly changing velocities. These conditions give rise to valuable "water-powers," many of which are already applied to industrial uses. Another consequence of the lack of uniformity in the hardness and compactness of the rock is that it has been "weathered" to a great and unusual depth. Excepting on the summits of the steeper hills, from which the weathered rock has been washed away as rapidly as formed, the effects of the weathering are noticeable to depths of from twenty to forty feet. Wells are generally sunk to these depths before hard rock is encountered. "Weathering" is the "breaking down, pulverization and decomposition of rocks and minerals by natural processes; that is, by the action of water, air, rain, wind, frost and such like natural agencies in operation constantly on the earth's surface." The "weathering" of rocks results in the formation of soil. The soil is, therefore, naturally very deep. Where it is protected from washing the depth to which it may be cultivated for farming purposes is practically unlimited.

The natural, inherent suitability of a soil for farming purposes depends in part upon the physical character and in part upon its chemical composition. Both of these are determined by the nature of the rock from which the soil was formed.

The principal minerals of which the granite rock is composed are quartz, feldspar and mica. True granite is a uniform, homogeneous mixture of these three minerals, each finely grained, compacted into a hard, uniform rock. Gneissoid granite contains the same three minerals, but it is not homogeneous in character; the minerals are coarsely grained and the rock is not so hard or compact as true granite. In true granite it is sometimes difficult to distinguish the minerals from each other by the unaided eye, but in the gneisses the large, coarse masses of each are generally easily distinguishable. In addition to quartz, feldspar and mica, other minerals in smaller quantities are sometimes among the components of the rock, such as hornblende, tourmaline, small veins of iron pyrites ("fool's gold"), etc., some of which are often prominently noticeable when the rock is freshly broken. Others, such as carbonate of lime, phosphate of lime, sulphate of lime, etc., occur in much smaller quantities, especially mixed through the soil formed of the rock when weathered. It is this heterogeneous character and coarse structure of the gneissoid rock that permits it to be weathered to such great depths.

The first effect of weathering is to crumble the rock The minerals are then separated and sorted by the action of water. The quartz crumbles into sand, and the mica into small, fine, glistening plates or scales. These are frequently noticeable in the dust by the roadside or in the beds and along the sides of small streams. Quartz simply forms sand; it cannot be further decomposed. The feldspar and mica (and other similar minerals) are, however, not only crumbled into fine particles but are actually decomposed. Thus, feldspar, which is composed chiefly of silica (silicic acid), alumina and potash, with small quantities of lime, soda, iron and other ingredients, decomposes under the action of weathering and produces sand (silica), clay (silicate of alumina and water) and silicate of potash principally, with small quantities of oxide of iron, lime and soda compounds, etc. Mica, which has a somewhat similar composition, produces on weathering similar results. The principal ingredients of the soil formed by the weathering of a gneissoid granite are, therefore, sand and clay ; and as the quantity of clay is large, such soils are usually clay soils. What may be called the *natural* soil of this region is, therefore, essentially a clay soil. As the quantity of iron in the feldspar, etc., is considerable, the oxide of iron formed during weathering gives the soil generally a decided red color. The sorting action of rainwater modifies to some extent the natural character of the soil in many places. Clay is lighter and finer than sand and is, therefore, more easily washed away. The larger streams of the country are therefore almost constantly more or less muddy from the quantity of fine clay which they carry, and the smaller streams are frequently so. This excessive washing away of the clay as compared with the sand results in the production of sandy soil. This is especially the case upon the tops and sides of the steeper hills and in "bottoms" where the velocity of a swiftly running stream is first checked. With the clay there is removed a good portion of the oxide of iron ; so, as the soils become sandy, they lose their red color and become "gray" soils. Organic matter—the remains of vegetation—upon the soil also affects the removal of the oxide of iron by solution, so that some of the soils are "gray" even when clayey.

The great bulk of the soils of the region are red clay lands, but sandy lands and gray lands are not uncommon. The numerous streams furnish considerable acreages of bottom lands of great fertility.

Even in the case of the distinctly clay lands the proportion of sand mixed with the clay is so great that they are rarely heavy or stiff, or in condition unsuited to easy and perfect tillage. The ease of cultivation of clay lands depends largely upon their freedom from excessive moisture. The rolling character of the lands of the country enables them to be properly drained without great difficulty. The hills, moreover, are not generally so steep or abrupt but that excessive washing may be prevented by ordinary and simple methods. Terracing for this purpose has found successful application almost universally.

Physically speaking, therefore, the soils of the region generally are admirably suited to farming operations, being deep, composed of thoroughly disintegrated materials, capable of easy drainage and protection from washing and of a character adapted to easy and economic cultivation.

The chemical composition of the soil may be illustrated by an analysis of a sample of the red clay land of the University farm. This farm is situated on a ridge-top, and the soil is less fertile than the average soil of the region of similar character. The sample represents the soil to a depth of twelve inches, and its composition is as follows:

Sand, clay, silicic acid, carbonic acid, etc	88.025
Water	4.038
Organic matter	4.593
Lime	0.292
Magnesia	0.270
Potash	0.781
Soda	0.685
Phosphoric acid	0.036
Sulphuric acid	0.076
Oxide of iron	1.204
	100.000

The composition of the soil per acre calculated from this analysis is as follows: One cubic foot of the soil weighed 81 pounds, and one acre, taken to a depth of 12 inches, weighed, accordingly, 3,528,000 pounds, as follows:

Sand, clay, silicic acid, carbonic acid, etc.,	3,105,730
Water	142,500
Organic matter	161,750
Lime	10,320
Magnesia	9,540
Potash	27,560
Soda	24,150
Phosphoric acid	1,260
Sulphuric acid	22,690
Oxide of iron	42,500
	3,528,000

Careful investigations have shown that given crops take from the soil certain quantities of certain mineral matters. The following may be given as illustrations.

Amounts (in pounds) of different substances used and required by plants in producing certain crops, including the roots, stem, leaves, fruit, grain, seed, etc., and all parts of the plant, representing the total demand made by the crop upon the soil.

1. COTTON, 200 POUNDS LINT PER ACRE.

Pounds.

Potash	32
Lime	40
Magnesia	12
Phosphoric acid	17
Other mineral matter	25

2. CORN, 50 BUSHELS SHELLED GRAIN.

Pounds.

Potash	77
Lime	35
Magnesia	20
Phosphoric acid	31
Other mineral matter	15

3. OATS, 20 BUSHELS.

Pounds.

Potash	20
Lime	7
Magnesia	5
Phosphoric acid	7
Other mineral matter	56

4. WHEAT, 10 BUSHELS.

Pounds.

Potash	10
Lime	4
Magnesia	3
Phosphoric acid	8
Other mineral matter	37

5. TIMOTHY HAY, 1 TON.

Pounds.

Potash	65
Lime	30
Magnesia	13
Phosphoric acid	16
Other mineral matter	100

6. RED CLOVER, 1 TON.

Pounds.

Potash	80
Lime	70
Magnesia	25
Phosphoric acid	20
Other mineral matter	25

Comparing the requirements of the crops with the actual capabilities of the soil, as indicated by the analysis, it is evident that, taken only to the depth of twelve inches, the ordinary soil of the region is abundantly provided with the mineral food necessary to produce luxuriant crops for many years without artificial fertilization. When it is remembered that the subsoil, down to the lowest depth that can possibly be reached by any plow, contains even larger quantities of plant food than are found in the surface soil, it is apparent that it is possible to maintain the natural fertility of the soil practically indefinitely. It is true that the fertility of a soil is mainly dependent upon the solubility or "availability" of the mineral plant food which it contains. In no soils may this availability be so readily or easily secured by judicious care of the land, green manuring, rotation of crops and other economic practices of good husbandry, as in soils of the character found in this region, the physical characteristics of which have been described, and which enable them to retain heat, air, moisture and the products of decay of organic matter, the natural agencies by which such availability is secured.

The general chemical character of the soil and its capacity to furnish mineral plant food may also be estimated from the composition of the minerals forming the rocks from which the soil was produced. All the minerals (excepting quartz) of the gneissoid granite underlying the soil of the metomorphic region are rich in potash, lime and magnesia, and contain the other necessary ingredients of plant food in good proportions. The soil formed by the weathering of such minerals is, therefore, necessarily a strong soil; that is, it contains plant food in abundance, its natural productive capacity is very great, and it responds readily to judicious tillage.

Another indication of the natural fertility of the soil is afforded by the character of the native vegetable growth. The timber of the region is mainly hard woods—oak, hickory, dogwood, etc.—a class of vegetation that demands from the soil much the same kind and amounts of mineral food as are required by ordinary cultivated crops.

It may be safely said, therefore, that the general character of the soil of the region is such as to yield to the husbandman full and rich returns for the labor of intelligent cultivation. As "proof of the pudding," attention is called to the agricultural statistics of the State given elsewhere, showing what the soil has actually been made to produce by careful culture.

As indicated above, the mineral matters of the soil, and of the underlying rock of this region, are mainly silicates—compounds of potash, lime, etc., with silica. These compounds are but slightly soluble in water (though competent to become sufficiently so for all purposes of plant growth). The water percolating through the soil and rock and collected in wells for drinking purposes, therefore contains but very small quantities of mineral matter in solution. Numerous analyses of the well waters of the region show that the amount of mineral matter held in solution is, on the average, not more than 2 grains per U. S. gallon. They are, therefore. "free-stone" waters of most excellent quality. The natural springs are of the same general character, and even the superficial streams, large and small, when freed from suspended sediment, are remarkably pure. Except where subject to local contamination, the organic purity of the natural waters is absolute. The extreme purity and the magnificent quality of the drinking waters of the region constitute one of its chief claims to healthfulness.

It has been previously noted that the oxide of iron which gives the red color to the soil is sometimes washed out (leaving "gray" land) by the percolating water when the quantity of organic (vegetable) matter upon or in the soil is large. This oxide of iron remains in solution until the water issues freely into the air. Iron, or "chalybeate" springs are, therefore, not infrequent.

This brief review of the geology of the region may serve, perhaps, to disclose the natural and sufficient basis for the claim that its salubrious climate, pure water and fertile soil fit it to be the home of a prosperous, sturdy and thrifty people.

The metamorphic region extends also into the northern parts of Alabama and South Carolina, giving soils of the same general character.

Climate and Health.

The climate of Georgia is affected by a variety of causes which modify the temperature usually accorded to this latitude. The same parallel that passes through Atlanta cuts Morocco, Algeria and Tunis, runs across Palestine, near Damascus, and penetrates Persia, Afghanistan and Thibet.

It is a well known fact that the western edges of continents have more humidity and fewer extremes of temperature than inland States. This accounts for the mild climate of England at a latitude which, on the Atlantic coast of America at New Foundland, or on the eastern coast of Asia at Kamchatka, is almost uninhabitable. Likewise the climate of the State of Washington, on our northwest coast, is mild, humid and without great extremes of heat or cold. In this it differs widely from the Dakotas and Montana, some hundreds of miles to the east.

In the same way large bodies of water extending inland modify climate. That of the Piedmont region is affected by the proximity of the Gulf of Mexico on one side and of the Atlantic Ocean on the other. The Gulf and the Caribbean Sea are the great reservoirs of moisture for the Gulf and South Atlantic States. The same causes affect the climate of Alabama, Florida and the Carolinas. In the northern part of these States the air of the mountainous regions is especially cool and bracing. Atlanta has a climate hardly equaled by any other city of 100,000 people on the continent. With no extreme cold in winter, it enjoys in summer cool nights, and days of less heat than Washington, Columbus, Cincinnati, Chicago, St. Louis or Kansas City. With an elevation of 1,052 feet above sea level, with other influences breaking the heat of summer, and with immunity from blizzards in winter, Atlanta, in point of climate, is the most favored city in the Union. It has never been visited by an epidemic, and this is true of almost the entire State, except on the coast and a few points of low altitude.

The advantages of the Piedmont region include something more than the physical comfort of man. The topography of the State, rising from the level pine lands of the South to the rolling surface of Middle Georgia, the hill country farther north, and the high mountains near the borders of North Carolina, gives a variety of climate and soil that makes room for an almost infinite variety of products. No State except Florida produces anything that will not grow in Georgia. Some tropical fruits grown in the lower part of the peninsula will not flourish here, but for the products of every other State, from Maine to California, Georgia has a hospitable soil.

Proximity to the Gulf of Mexico, which has been called "the great weather breeder" for this part of the continent, gives a supply of moisture that never leaves a total failure of crops. On this subject Gen. A. W. Greeley, late chief of the United States Weather Bureau, says in his book entitled "American Weather:"

"The variability of rainfall is an important question for all agricultural interests, since an annual rainfall of 20 inches may mean a fall of 30 inches for several years, followed by years of 15 inches or less. * * * It is noticeable that the percentage of deviation is exceedingly small along the Atlantic seacoast and on the shores of the Gulf of Mexico. This small variability is a reliable indication that such sections are free from prolonged and disastrous droughts."

The wide range of Georgia's climate is such that wheat is profitably grown in North and Middle Georgia while the middle and southern counties produce a fine quality of sugar cane and the coast abounds in rice. Here the products of the temperate zone and the tropics meet. This year wheat and sugar cane grew within hailing distance of each other on the Atlanta and West Point Railroad.

TEMPERATURE AND RAINFALL.

The following tables, compiled by Mr. Park Morrill, of the United States Weather Bureau, will show the variety of the climate in Georgia, varying in temperature and rainfall, with the latitude and elevation above the sea. The data upon which these figures are based consist of observations covering a period of eight years. The first table shows the temperature and the second the rainfall. By a comparison of the two it will be seen that at the elevated points in North Georgia, where the temperature was low, the rainfall was high. The lowest temperature and the highest rainfall were at Rabun Gap, which has an elevation of 2,220 feet above the sea, and the next lowest temperature and the next highest rainfall were at Gainesville, with an elevation of 1,222 feet. In direct contrast with these was the lightest rainfall, with one of the highest temperatures at Augusta, where the altitude is only 147 feet above sea level. Similar figures are noticed at Macon and Americus, which are but a little above Augusta in elevation.

TABLE I.—NORMAL TEMPERATURE FOR GEORGIA.

No. of Years of Record.	STATION.	Jan.	Feb.	Mar.	Apr.	May.	June.	July.	Aug.	Sept.	Oct.	Nov.	Dec.	Annual
10	Americus	49.4	54.3	58.7	68.1	74.8	80.8	83.0	81.0	77.1	68.9	58.6	53.3	67.4
13	Athens	41.7	46.7	50.3	61.3	69.0	75.5	77.6	76.1	71.2	60.3	50.4	44.4	60.4
24	Atlanta	41.6	46.6	51.2	60.7	68.0	74.7	78.0	75.8	70.4	60.0	50.9	44.1	60.2
48	Augusta	47.0	51.1	55.7	64.6	72.4	78.9	81.7	79.6	74.3	64.0	53.9	47.4	64.2
9	Brunswick	53.0	55.6	61.1	67.6	75.2	79.9	82.8	81.7	77.8	70.3	61.4	55.4	68.5
16	Gainesville	41.1	44.2	51.7	60.5	68.1	74.9	78.1	75.6	70.0	60.6	49.6	43.3	59.8
12	LaGrange	44.0	49.9	53.6	63.3	70.9	76.3	81.2	78.7	74.3	65.2	52.6	45.7	63.0
15	Macon	47.3	50.1	55.6	64.8	72.8	79.4	81.5	80.2	75.6	65.4	54.4	46.7	64.5
10	Milledgeville	43.7	50.3	53.3	63.8	71.3	77.5	80.7	78.2	72.9	62.3	53.1	49.2	63.0
9	Rabun Gap	36.4	42.4	46.2	55.7	63.4	68.8	72.3	71.0	65.7	59.3	45.6	39.0	55.5
12	Rome	40.4	46.6	51.8	62.3	69.5	75.6	79.6	77.4	71.2	62.9	50.1	42.9	60.9
12	Saint Mary's	52.5	55.5	60.1	66.9	73.3	78.8	80.4	80.1	77.1	68.2	59.2	52.4	67.0
44	Savannah	51.5	54.8	59.3	66.7	73.9	79.3	81.8	80.5	76.1	66.7	57.8	52.6	66.8
10	Thomson	44.9	50.5	54.1	62.4	70.3	76.8	81.4	79.2	75.0	65.7	53.4	46.4	63.3

TABLE II.—NORMAL PRECIPITATION FOR GEORGIA.

No. of Years of Record.	STATION.	Jan.	Feb.	Mar.	Apr.	May.	June.	July.	Aug.	Sept.	Oct.	Nov.	Dec.	Annu
11	Americus	4.50	3.23	5.31	3.57	3.34	5.44	5.46	5.42	3.04	1.79	2.55	3.18	46.83
18	Athens	5.97	5.38	5.29	3.53	4.29	5.01	4.90	4.83	3.88	2.34	3.47	3.87	52.76
28	Atlanta	5.24	5.29	5.86	4.33	3.66	4.28	3.79	4.48	3.88	2.31	3.79	4.72	51.63
28	Augusta	4.32	3.78	5.16	3.24	3.14	4.17	4.69	4.64	3.79	2.43	2.92	3.72	46.01
18	Gainesville	6.37	6.54	6.60	3.80	3.71	5.15	4.62	6.42	4.78	2.80	3.92	5.66	60.37
12	LaGrange	4.58	4.76	6.42	3.67	2.98	4.86	4.69	5.03	2.67	2.39	3.12	4.90	50.12
18	Macon	4.05	3.86	5.79	4.36	3.27	3.73	4.88	3.97	3.24	1.87	3.05	4.34	46.41
10	Milledgeville	5.48	4.49	5.88	1.92	3.44	4.41	5.75	5.69	3.73	2.59	2.17	3.92	49.36
9	Rabun Gap	7.26	6.34	7.60	5.23	4.88	4.59	4.59	5.98	4.73	6.28	5.11	5.76	68.35
13	Rome	5.71	4.64	5.87	4.28	3.20	4.33	3.70	4.00	2.50	2.22	3.52	4.10	48.16
44	Savannah	3.26	2.76	3.86	2.86	3.95	5.59	6.75	8.04	5.67	2.98	2.00	3.31	51.03
11	St. Mary's	2.57	3.37	3.55	2.92	4.60	6.44	4.76	5.80	8.92	3.37	2.43	3.51	52.24
10	Thomson	5.42	3.32	5.46	3.39	4.00	4.46	4.51	4.78	2.62	3.14	2.87	3.59	47.56
8	Walthourville	3.30	2.18	2.52	3.19	2.91	5.18	5.78	5.87	7.12	3.56	1.99	...	...

DAY AND NIGHT TEMPERATURES.

The following table, compiled from the records of two years in the United States Signal Office in Atlanta, gives the contrast between the day and night (maximum and minimum) temperatures of each month, with the highest and lowest for each month. It will be seen that as a rule the summers in Georgia have cool nights, which fortify the system against the heat of the day. The extremes of heat and cold were not so great as in other parts of the country far to the north of this region.

TABLE III.—SHOWING THE DIFFERENCE BETWEEN DAY AND NIGHT TEMPERATURES.

	ATLANTA.				AUGUSTA.				SAVANNAH.			
	Mean Maximum	Mean Minimum	Highest	Lowest	Mean Maximum	Mean Minimum	Highest	Lowest	Mean Maximum	Mean Minimum	Highest	Lowest
January	45.7 43.6	30.9 28.4	65 65	17 8	51 47.9	17 29.6	69 68	23 12	55.7 53.2	30.4 35.4	72 71	19 18
February	56 53.2	39.7 39.1	65 70	23 30	60.2 59.4	41.8 42.2	70 74	28 31	63.1 65.9	45.8 47.8	75 87	32 34
March	57.3 60.5	38.7 42.2	77 79	17 18	61.7 61.4	43 44.2	79 81	25 23	65.6 65.7	46.8 48.4	83 81	27 26
April	68.8 73.8	49.2 54.6	82 84	32 39	78 80.2	52.3 57.6	85 91	35 42	74.2 70.4	56.8 60 7	85 89	42 51
May	78 76.2	59.5 58.2	88 90	45 47	85 5 81.6	60.6 59.8	92 94	47 49	81.8 82	63.9 64	91 92	51 54
June	85.3 82.9	67 65.4	93 88	62 57	87 4 86.4	69.1 67.8	95 93	65 59	84.6 87	70.5 70	96 93	65 63
July	84.1 90.7	68.6 70.6	91 93	59 66	87.3 93	71.0 72	97 98	64 67	88.6 93	72 74	97 100	65 69
August	83 9 85.7	68.5 68.3	91 91	62 62	89.1 86.9	71.1 70.2	96 92	68 64	89.8 87.1	72.7 71.5	96 92	70 67
September	78.9 81.7	61.1 64.4	85 90	50 55	82.1 85	63.7 66.5	90 95	51 55	81.8 86	68.1 70	90 97	59 59
October	69.3 71.9	49.5 53.3	84 82	36 35	71.5 74.5	50.1 53.3	90 85	32 33	71.9 75.5	56.6 57	89 85	41 40
November	67.6 59	40.1 49.7	75 76	18 24	62.6 61.4	42 41.7	81 83	26 23	64.7 67.2	46.6 46 9	79 82	30 30
December	54.5 49.5	39.6 39.2	65 69	25 13	60.4 57.8	40.5 38.6	73 76	22 23	60.4 62.2	46.7 44 4	77 77	27 25

NOTE.—The two figures given for each month are for two successive years, showing the variation. Mean maximum gives day, and mean minimum, night temperature.

Concerning the relation of climate to plant life an interesting discussion took place in the Georgia Horticultural Society at Athens in 1893. Dr. P. J. Berckmans, of Augusta, the president of the society, said: "Georgia not only extends over several degrees of latitude, from south to north, but its elevation from the sea line to the mountains corresponds with the latitude, accentuating its climatological effect and rendering its area, as adapted to various forms of life, a singularly comprehensive one, with an enormous range. We hence established for our catalogue of fruits a mountain region, classifying for that region, with its peculiar climate, those fruits best adapted to it, and so on for the middle region, southern region and coast region, all with greatly differing features and climates. * * * Here is a territory stretched over five actual degrees of latitude, the topography of which easily exaggerates these five into ten."

In the same discussion Dr. Cary, superintendent of fisheries for Georgia, stated that he had taken the temperature of the gulf stream off the South Florida coast and there it was 79 degrees and so warm that in midwinter bathing was practicable.

MORTUARY RECORD.

Alabama	14.20	per 1,000 population.
Florida	11.72	" " "
Georgia	13.97	" " "
North Carolina	15.39	" " "
South Carolina	15.80	" " "
Mississippi	12.89	" " "
Illinois	14.63	" " "
Indiana	15.78	" " "
Iowa	11.93	" " "
Kansas	15.22	" " "
Michigan	12.06	" " "
Minnesota	11.57	" " "
New York	17.38	" " "
Pennsylvania	14.92	" " "

In the country the average mortality of whites is 14, and of blacks 17 per thousand. Taking whites alone, the mortality in the Piedmont States averages about 12 per 1,000.

A noticeable fact is that the mortality of the negroes

almost doubles in the cities. From 17 per thousand in the country, it runs to 30 or forty in cities. In Charleston it is above forty. This is due to the fact that the negroes in cities occupy the worst locations, and live in very unsanitary conditions. When it is known that in the last twenty years, and especially in the last five or ten years, the blacks have been flocking to the cities, it may be understood why the increase of the negroes during the past decade has only been about half that of the whites. The census of 1890 shows that in the Piedmont States the negro population increased 13 per cent., while in the same period the whites increased 25 per cent.

Agriculture.

In the census year the North Central States, without Missouri, produced $1,000,000,000 of farm products on land worth seven times as much. In the same year the eighteen Southern States produced $873,000,000 on land worth less than four times as much. That is to say, the earth yields to the Southern farmer 25 per cent. on his capital every year, while it yields to his brother in the North only 14 per cent. If we include as capital the value of the machinery and live stock, the difference becomes greater, in favor of the Southern farmer, for of implements, machinery and live stock the North Central States have $1,350,000,000 as against $600,000,000 in the Southern States. The account stands thus:

	INVESTMENT.	RETURN.
North Central States	$8,400,000,000	$1,010,000,000
Southern States	3,800,000,000	873,000,000

Of the Southern crop, Georgia produces nearly a tenth. On land valued at $152,000,000 she raised products worth $83,000,000 On lands valued five times as high Indiana produced only a little more—$94,000,000! Georgia soil returns to the husbandman 55 per cent. on the value of his land, while Indiana gives him only 13 per cent.! South Carolina gives 52 per cent. and Alabama 60 per cent! This does not mean that the Southern lands are more productive than those of the North and West, but simply that, in proportion to their valuation, the farm lands of the Southeast are the most productive in the Union. They yield a return from two to four times as large as others o the capital invested, and do it with less labor and without an arduous battle with the elements. The Southern farmer does not have to run a race with the blizzard to harvest his crops.

These cheap lands may be made to produce double what they do. Mr. McCollum, the superintendent of the Western and Atlantic Railway, has a farm in North Georgia on which he made last year seventy-five bushels of corn to the acre. A long list of equally good crops in the cereals, grasses, cotton, potatoes and cane will be found at the end of this article. It shows what the land will do when put to its best by thorough tillage. The red lands in the hilly region of Georgia, Alabama and the Carolinas may be brought up to this point with little expense by successive crops of leguminous plants, cut and fed to cattle and the stubble turned under the sod. The peas alternate with grain or cotton, and the cattle feeding on the hay or peas take on marketable flesh, while they leave a fertilizer behind. After the oil, now amounting to twenty millions a year, is taken from the seed, it leaves first-class food for cattle, and after the cattle take enough from it to put a couple of hundred pounds on each carcass, they return it to the soil with interest. The old plan was to put the cotton seed back in the furrow. Now we take from it first oil and then beef, and return it to the ground a better fertilizer than it was before. Some gentlemen connected with the Southern Cotton Oil Mills fed ten thousand cattle on cotton seed meal and hulls after the oil had been extracted. They sold the cattle for a profit of $20,000 over and above the cost of the animals and the feed, taking no account of the manure. To the farmer the last item would have been worth as much as the other profit.

By such methods, radically different from the old system, the lands of Georgia may be made to double their product. A man who buys a farm at the present price and builds it up by this means will have a good return on his capital from the first, and will find the principal doubled in a few years.

The dairy and poultry products of Georgia are worth half as much as the cotton crop. It is a picturesque contrast. The horses and mules about equal the cows in number, and the men about equal the women. Yet with all their labor and toil the men and horses and mules do not much surpass the women and cows and chickens. When it comes to clear profit on the amount of money invested, there is no comparison. The interesting part of it is that while cotton is going lower and lower, milk, butter, eggs and chickens are firm and advancing. The cows are only rated at six millions, but they produce fifty million gallons of milk and fifteen million pounds of butter, worth more than double that sum, with the calves thrown in for good measure. The broods which eight million chickens and turkeys bring are worth more than all the colts foaled in Georgia, and the eleven million dozen eggs are worth as much more. The chickens and eggs are worth as much as the wheat crop, yet the fowls thrive on chaff and gleanings. The value of the grain crops is not fully measured till we get the returns for chickens and eggs.

These plain facts, taken from the cold type of the census, read like a romance, and it is a wonder that these small products, which come in as the farmer's perquisite, have so little attention. Though it seems strange that the dairy products of Georgia should come so near the cotton crop, which dominates everything, we could easily make it double the cotton crop. Ohio's dairy products, not including cheese, are worth two of Georgia's cotton crops, though they have to house cows three times as long in Ohio as in Georgia, and when the cattle do go out to graze, it is on land that costs five to ten times as much, though the grass does not grow there so well or so long as in the Piedmont region.

BERMUDA GRASS.

A great variety of grasses flourish here, but the Bermuda grass is to Georgia what blue grass is to Kentucky. It has made Middle Georgia a great region for live stock and has shown high merit as a hay crop. The following description of it is quoted from the Hand-book of Georgia, issued by the State Agricultural Department in 1885, but now out of print:

"No State in all our wide domain can offer in the same space larger inducements to the stock raiser or dairyman. Beginning in January at the seacoast, we have the tender salt marsh, which makes no insignificant reliance at that season. By the 1st of March the open wood grasses appear. These consist of the piney woods sedge, called wire-grass, with innumerable patches of switch cane, which keep cattle fat during the most inclement months. Besides these the Spanish long moss, a striking peculiarity of low coast latitudes, all through the winter continues succulent and nourishing and is eaten greedily by all stock.

"But better far than any or all these is the world-renowned grass Cynodon Dactolon, known in India as the "Daub" or sacred grass, and throughout the Southern States as Bermuda grass. It is not propagated by its seed, and indeed it is not thought to mature its seed in the United States. It takes deep hold in the soil with its mass of roots and covers the surface with a superficial network of twinelike runners, which make one of the most compact swards we know.

"While this grass requires some nursing on uplands of moderate fertility to give it the necessary height for mowing, it invariably attains on low lands, or high lands in good heart, a growth which makes mowing by machinery an easy matter.

"A peculiar advantage of Bermuda grass is that in the lower portion of the State the vetch grows luxuriantly in the very thickest of the sward, while in the upper sections the white clover will also put up through the interstices of the runners and give a good nip for sheep or Jerseys during the winter months. The farmer who knows what it costs to feed a herd of cattle will know the value of a grass which men say can never be got rid of, that ties the most washing soil together, that catches and holds every particle of manure that is dropped on it, which gives a pasturage every day in the year in lower Georgia and nine months in the upper part, which restores a worn soil better than blue grass and on rich land will yield 20,000 pounds of hay, which by a strict and authentic analysis contains 14 per cent of albumenoids. This, upon the high authority of the late Dr. St. Julian Ravenel, makes the hay of Bermuda more valuable than that of the celebrated timothy. In fattening qualities and healthfulness it seems the very best pasturage for sheep. There can be no question of its superiority as a grass and hay producer to anything known in Europe or the United States."

Space does not suffice to even catalogue the grasses which grow and thrive in Georgia. There is a long list running from red clover to wire grass. The latter is a growth indigenous to the piney woods of the Southern part of the State, covering nearly half of the 137 counties, appearing early in spring in the forest, the tender shoots of the wire grass furnishing an excellent pasturage for cattle or sheep. Most of the sheep raised in Georgia are in the wiregrass region and cattle have been pastured in the forest by the thousand. There they find food little inferior to that of the Western plains, and in the mild climate of Southern Georgia, protected from cold winds by the endless canopy of the pine tops, they escape the stress of weather which kills immense herds on the Western plains.

SAMPLE CROPS.

The following statements of crops made by thorough culture in Georgia were reported to the State Agricultural Department upon well authenticated proof, and may be accepted as reliable. It is understood that this is not the average, but a sample of good farming:

Thomas County—R. H. Hardaway, 119 bushels corn on one acre, 1875. E. T. Davis, 96½ bushels oats on one acre. After harvesting the oats, made 800 pounds seed cotton on the same acre. John J. Parker, 694 gallons cane syrup.

Brooks County—Wiley W. Groover produced with two horses on 126½ acres, without commercial fertilizers, cotton, corn, oats, peas, cane and potatoes worth $3,258. Cost of production $1,045; profit $2,213. Joseph Hodges, 2,700 pounds seed cotton on one acre. Wm. Boden 600 gallons syrup, J. Bower 500 bushels sweet potatoes, J. O. Morton 75 bushels oats, T. W. Jones 480 gallons syrup, each on one acre.

Bulloch County—3,500 pounds seed cotton on one acre by Samuel Groover.

Clay County—Mr. Hodge made 4,500 pounds seed cotton on one acre.

Schley County—J. R. Respess, 500 bushels of oats on five acres. Also 15,000 pounds seed cotton on five acres.

Berrien County—H. T. Peeples, 800 bushels sweet potatoes on one acre pine land.

Spalding County—G. J. Drake, 74 bushels of corn on one acre, S. W. Bloodworth 137 bushels on one acre.

Carroll County—John Bonner 3 bales of cotton on one acre. R. H. Springer 9 bales on five acres without manure and 98 bales on one hundred acres by using fertilizers, S. W. Leak 40½ bushels of wheat on one acre.

Wilkes—123 bushels of corn on one acre. Also on one acre 137 bushels of oats.

Burke County—Dr. Wm. Jones 480 gallons syrup on one acre, Wesley Jones 3 bales of cotton.

Washington County—T. C. Warthen 5 bales of cotton on one acre and a ninth.

Pike County—R. M. Brooks 500 bushels of rice on five acres.

Hancock County—R. B. Baxter, first cutting of clover, harvested 4,862 pounds dry hay per acre.

Crawford County—A. J. Preston 4,000 pounds seed cotton on one acre and 115 bushels of corn on another.

Greene County—Dr. T. P. Jones 5 tons of clover hay per acre in one season at two cuttings.

Bibb County—Patrick Long made 8,646 pounds of native crabgrass hay on one acre after he had gathered a crop of cabbages from the same land in June.

Spalding County—S. W. Leak, on one acre from which he had harvested 40 bushels of wheat in June, gathered 10,720 pounds of peavine hay, making in one year on a single acre $299. J. T. Manley 115 bushels of oats on one acre.

Coweta County—Wm. Smith 2,200 pounds of seed cotton per acre on ten acres.

Gordon County—Richard Peters 14 tons of Lucern on three acres.

Walker County—Capt. C. W. Howard bought land on Lookout Mountain for 25 cents an acre, and on one acre, without manure, with one hoeing, made 108 bushels of Irish potatoes which sold in Atlanta for $97.

Cherokee County—Thomas Smith made 104 bushels of corn on one acre.

Bibb County—John Dyer made 398 bushels of sweet potatoes on one acre, and sold them for $298. Cost of culture only $8.

Fulton County—Haddon P. Redding made 400 bushels

of yams on one acre and sold them for $1 per bushel in Atlanta.

In 1884 George W. Scott & Co., of Atlanta, offered $800 in gold for the best yield of cotton and corn made on land enriched by the Scott fertilizers. Seventy-five farmers contested for the cotton prize and they averaged 774 pounds of lint cotton per acre. The highest yield was 1,545 pounds of lint cotton or three and a half bales per acre. There were sixteen corn planters, who averaged 81 bushels per acre. The highest yield was 116½ bushels.

The next year the same firm offered prizes for wheat. The three premium acres averaged 40 bushels each. The highest was 65 bushels.

At the same time premiums were offered for the best yields of oats. The three prize acres averaged 113 bushels and the highest was 132.

Below are the totals of the principal crops in Georgia, Alabama, South Carolina and North Carolina:

THE CORN CROP OF 1892.

STATE.	BUSHELS.	VALUE.
Alabama	30,666,000	$15,946,412
Georgia	32,992,000	18,475,481
South Carolina	16,713.000	9,526,187
North Carolina	25,347,000	13,687,435

The corn crop of Georgia this year will probably be 40,000,000 bushels.

THE WHEAT CROP OF 1892.

STATE.	BUSHELS.	VALUE.
Alabama	306,000	$ 284,134
Georgia	1,474,000	1,326,938
North Carolina	5,090,000	4,530,356
South Carolina	938,000	872,390

The wheat crop of Georgia this year will probably be 3,000,000 bushels.

AGRICULTURE.

THE OAT CROP OF 1892.

STATE.	BUSHELS.	VALUE.
Alabama	3,721,000	$1,897,742
Georgia	6,090,000	3,166,673
South Carolina	3,682,000	1,914,708
North Carolina	5,332,000	2,399,515

THE COTTON CROP OF 1890.

	BALES.
Alabama	914,000
Georgia	1,191,919
North Carolina	336,249
South Carolina	746,798

HORSES IN 1892.

	NUMBER.	VALUE.
Alabama	121,446	$8,485,421
Georgia	104,309	8,450,807
South Carolina	60,629	5,285,433
North Carolina	131,866	10,366,953

MULES IN 1892.

	NUMBER.	VALUE.
Alabama	136,095	$11,783,744
Georgia	157,257	14,916,959
South Carolina	86,403	8,257,164
North Carolina	100,185	8,828,881

MILCH COWS IN 1892.

	NUMBER.	VALUE.
Alabama	311,774	$4,676,610
Georgia	354,583	6,382,494
South Carolina	155,009	3,148,233
North Carolina	269,379	4,741,070

OXEN AND OTHER CATTLE IN 1892.

	NUMBER.	VALUE.
Alabama	445,007	$4,006,179
Georgia	569,200	5,613,450
South Carolina	204,126	2,629,043
North Carolina	390,446	4,526,990

SHEEP IN 1892.

	NUMBER.	VALUE.
Alabama	269,292	$443,927
Georgia	383,017	673,956
South Carolina	89,073	167,903
North Carolina	390,261	710,275

SWINE IN 1892.

	NUMBER.	VALUE.
Alabama	1,499,554	$4,356,205
Georgia	1,691,275	5,692,832
South Carolina	684,065	2,827,924
North Carolina	1,253,136	4,639,735

We have fewer horses by 25 per cent. than in 1860, but we have from 25 to 50 per cent. more mules, cows and sheep. We have not quite so many swine. Of all these things we have about double what we had in 1870. The war swept away nearly half our live stock, but since 1870 we have renewed the supply and about 25 per cent. over.

Truck Farming.

The census bulletin on truck farming, issued March 19, 1891, shows that the value of such products for all the States during the census year was $76,517,155, produced on 534,440 acres.

Of this amount the truck farms in the vicinity of New York and Philadelphia produced $21,102,521, more than any of the geographical groups. This was raised on 108,135 acres. Next came the Central States with a product of $15,432,223, and the South Atlantic States with $13,183,516, grown on 111,441 acres. The South Atlantic States, embracing most of the Piedmont region, stand third in the groups of States in the value of truck products. These figures show that the average yield was $118 per acre, while that of the Central States is $143 per acre. The great cities of New York and Philadelphia, paying high prices for fruits and vegetables, the truck farmers of that vicinity realize $195 per acre. The value of truck products per acre is thus to a degree regulated by the size of the cities it supplies. The growing cities of Atlanta, Savannah, Charleston, Augusta, Mobile, Memphis, Montgomery, Birmingham, Columbia, Macon, Raleigh and Wilmington make this industry more valuable each year, but the strong point of the fruit and truck industry in the Piedmont region is quick access to the great cities of the East, where the early fruits and vegeables find a ready market at good prices.

It is noticeable that the States of the Piedmont region, called the South Atlantic group, produce in truck products about three times as much as the States of the Mississippi valley, and about six times as much as the Pacific coast. The actual figures, by groups of States, are as follows:

	ACRES.	VALUE.
New England	6,838	$ 3,184,218
New York and Philadelphia	108,135	21,102,521
Peninsula	25,714	2,413,648
Norfolk	45,375	4,692,852
Baltimore	37,181	3,784,696
South Atlantic	111,444	13,183,516
Mississippi Valley	36,180	4,982,579
Southwest	36,889	4,979,783
Central	107,414	15,432,223
Northwest	1,083	204,791
Mountain	3,833	531,976
Pacific Coast	14,357	2,024,345

Two items in the report from Mobile show the growth of the truck industry in Alabama. In 1880 it sent out 30,874 barrels of potatoes, which yielded $61,748. In 1890 the shipment was 78,924 barrels, worth $138,117. Only 1,242 crates of cabbage, worth $6,216, were shipped in 1880, while in 1890 there were 58,309 crates, which brought $174,927.

While the census does not give the shipments by years from Georgia it says under the report from Mobile above quoted: "Equally good returns could be given for other distributing points in Southern trucking districts, such as Savannah, Ga., Charleston, S. C., Jacksonville, Fla., etc. The matter is summed up thus by the census bulletin above referred to:

"Nearly 75 per cent. of the truck produced in the United States comes from a belt of country along the Atlantic coast, lying east of a line drawn from Augusta, Me., to Macon, Ga., from Southern Georgia, Alabama and Florida; along the north and south lines of railroad in the Mississippi valley from the gulf to Chicago, St. Louis and Kansas City, and from the celery districts of Michigan."

The truck crops of the South Atlantic States go by

rail or steamer to New York, Boston, Philadelphia, Baltimore, Cincinnati and Chicago.

WATERMELONS.

The Georgia watermelon is the king of all the trucker's products. In 1890 there were 55,726 acres planted in melons in the South Atlantic States, out of 114,381 in the entire country, the larger part of the crop being in Georgia. The magnitude of the Georgia crop may be understood when it is known that it made 10,000 carloads.

COST OF LABOR AND FERTILIZERS.

The labor cost on leading vegetables is little more than half as much per acre in the South Atlantic States as in New England and in the vicinity of New York and Philadelphia. For instance, the cost of labor per acre on asparagus is $34.27 in New England; $36.46 in New York and Philadelphia; and $21.25 in the South Atlantic States. On beans it is for these districts respectively $42, $35 and $8.07. On cabbage it is $36.25, $26.20 and $15.95. On watermelons it is $24, $14.29 and $7.10. On Irish potatoes $16, $16.25 and $16.40. It costs $75 an acre to cultivate tomatoes in New England and only $22.50 in the Piedmont region. The average wages of men on truck farms in New England is $1.25 per day; in the South Atlantic States it is 85 cents.

The cost of fertilizers per acre on the truck farms of the Piedmont region ranges from 40 to 70 per cent. of the cost in New England. Beans which cost $30 to fertilize in the neighborhood of Boston cost $7.25 in the South Atlantic States; cabbage that costs in fertilizers $67.85 in New England is raised in the Piedmont region with $22.75 worth of fertilizers.

The cost of labor and fertilizers in the South is much less in proportion to the amount realized per acre. Hence the margin of profit is greater.

Fruit Growing in the Piedmont Region.

BY MR. G. H. MILLER, OF THE EXCELSIOR NURSERY, ROME, GA.

Before giving our observations and convictions in regard to fruit growing in the Piedmont region, allow us to say that we have been in the nursery and fruit business for more than a quarter of a century and have studied the problem of fruit growing in the South for nine years. We have made observations in many different localities in the Piedmont region, as well as in the region south of that, and the statements which we will give are our honest convictions, and we think they are very conservative.

In fruit growing in the South, as well as in the same business in any other location in our country, the problems of location, varieties, culture, handling, transportation and markets are essential factors contributing to success or failure. The commercial fruit grower in the South needs as much brain and as varied a range of knowledge as the fruit grower in any other section of our country, but we do not hesitate to make the general proposition that fruit culture in Georgia promises as satisfactory returns to those who will cultivate and handle their fruits in an intelligent and careful manner as could be received from the same application of industry and skill in any of the most favored fruit regions in our country. We even think that the percentage of profit will be larger here than in any other location that can be named, because less capital is required in starting fruit growing, as lands are very much cheaper than fruit lands in any other section.

APPLES.

First, in regard to apple culture in the Piedmont region. This is an industry which has not as yet been fully developed, except in a few localities. All over the Piedmont region there are elevated table lands, as on Sand Mountain, Lookout and all the little ranges that run through Northern Georgia and East Tennessee, extending into North Carolina. On these table lands, the soils of which are usually sandy loam, can be grown as fine apples as in the apple regions of Western New York, Michigan or Missouri. We sent Rome Beauties grown on some of these table lands to the Agricultural Department at Washington City last year, and they were pronounced by them the most highly colored and the finest specimens of that variety they had ever seen. We are familiar with the Rome Beauty as grown in Southern Ohio, its original home, and must say that the specimens we received from the Piedmont region were the most beautiful samples of that variety we have ever seen. So it is with numerous other varieties that we have seen grown on these table lands. We know parties who are cultivating apples on these table lands intelligently, and they are making money. They have no trouble in marketing their apples, hardly ever selling them for less than $1 per bushel, and sometimes as high at $6 per barrel. There is no question but that on these table lands and in many of the coves around the base of the mountains there are admirable locations for apple culture. As we intimated, this field is all open to the intelligent cultivator who will occupy it, as when you find one apple orchard properly managed you might travel fifty miles before you would find another, anywhere in this region, unless in a few localities.

Then as to market for apples, we have it right at our doors. All the South bordering on the Gulf States is not suitable for apple culture, unless it be a few early varieties, and this market must be supplied from other sections. The holiday trade in our cities consumes train loads of apples every year shipped from the North, which can be grown of as good quality right here at home. We do not know of a more inviting field for investment than commercial apple growing in this section of the country. Of course, it is understood that the apple industry as well as any other business, to be successful, must have intelligence and industry applied to it.

Then again, early apples can be grown in this section to supply the Northern market, apples that will come into the market of the Northern cities immediately after the strawberry crops in their latitude are exhausted. There is a great demand for apples suitable for cooking and for dessert. What few growers are endeavoring to supply this market are getting very fine prices for their apples.

In this section of the South, every season, a great many apples are hauled by ox teams from sixty to 100 miles to the cities and sold, after all the jolting on the road for days, for $1 per bushel, from orchards managed strictly on the "let alone" system, where such a thing as hand-picking, sorting and barrelling apples is utterly unknown. Any one interested in apple culture can easily satisfy himself by a visit to this section of the wonderful opportunities which are afforded for successful commercial apple growing.

PEACHES.

In this section of country there are ranges of hills of a lower elevation, the tops of which are usually table lands of varying extent and from one to perhaps three miles in width on which peaches succeed admirably. They will do well on the higher table lands, but are not so sure a crop, owing to being caught by late spring frosts. But there appears to be a certain range of ridges and of table lands on some of these mountains, of height varying from 250 to 300 feet above the level of the valleys adjacent, which is called the frostless belt, and on these elevations peaches are a sure crop. At this elevation there is considerable iron in the soil and peaches are of finer quality and more highly colored than those grown anywhere else, not excepting even the far-famed peach region of Middle Georgia, where large orchards are being planted. We do not say a word against the peach region of Middle Georgia, but confine our remarks more especially to the Piedmont region, as we have studied that more carefully. We have compared some varieties grown in the Piedmont region with the same varieties grown in Middle Georgia and invariably found those grown in the Piedmont region larger and more highly colored. Also having the advantage of being much nearer market, reaching the markets of the North at least twelve to fifteen hours sooner than those further South.

Here again this region affords great inducements to peach culture from the fact that lands suitable for peach culture can be bought at a very low price.

Not only are the Northern markets open to peach growers in this section, but the Southern market along the gulf region is open to our late peaches. That market is at present scarcely supplied at all with late peaches. These varieties can be grown in the Piedmont region and shipped south at a large profit, as there is always a demand for them in the proper season.

Georgia peaches have already established a reputation for quality. In all the Northern markets they are quoted at the very top. The intelligent consumer asks the question: "Have you any Georgia peaches?" " We do not want California fruit if we can get Georgia fruit " is a very common expression heard in front of the fruit stands in the Northern cities.

If fruit growing in the North is profitable on lands worth from $50 to $100 per acre, it must certainly be more profitable on lands in the South worth from $5 to $10 per acre, and where labor can always be had at a cheap rate. Then again, we have no expense of irrigation, as in California, and we do not have to cross a continent to get to markets.

This section of country is also admirably adapted to the culture of plums, especially the Wild Goose and the new varieties of Japanese plums, which have proved a complete success in this section, and can be shipped to any Northern market or to Canada with perfect success. The same statement will apply to grapes, for which all this section is admirably adapted, and as they can be got into the Northern markets before grapes in that section are ripe they command a better price than Northern grapes do. Anyone who will take the pains to investigate the adaptation of this section to fruit culture in all its branches can be convinced that it is pre-eminently suited for the fruit industry in all of its branches.

Not only to the commercial fruit grower does this section of the South offer special inducements, but to the home-seeker, who wishes to establish for himself and family a home where he can enjoy all the fruits of the temperate zone, where he can surround his home with everything that is beautiful, and that will cause his children to "look with lovers' eyes on their home," that where'er they may wander they will always think of home as the dearest spot on earth to them—"the brightest oasis on the pathway of life." In this region they can secure for themselves homes, of which the wanderer who leans over their humble gate "will think the while,

"Oh, that for me some home like this would smile."

This is a section of beautiful and magnificent landscapes, of which the eye never wearies, and when it shall be settled up more closely, and homes improved by ornamental planting, and the fields and hills dotted over with orchards, it will indeed be almost a paradise.

IN OTHER SECTIONS OF THE STATE.

Fruitgrowing is even a larger industry in Middle and Southern Georgia than in the northern part of the State. At the State Horticultural Society's meeting in Athens, in 1893, Mr. S. H. Rumph, of Marshallville, who is the largest grower in Georgia, reported that more than 1,000,000 of peach trees had been planted in two years in his neighborhood, and, though the crop was not so good as usual, 140 car loads had been shipped from there that summer. The net return was $500 to $800 per car load, according to quality.

Dr. H. H. Cary reported from LaGrange that there were 1,200 acres in fruit trees in that vicinity and the area was constantly increasing. About Quitman, in Southern Georgia, Mr. John Tillman reported commercial orchards covering 3,500 acres.

These are but a few localities. Most fruits grow everywhere. There are large commercial orchards in Houston, Floyd, Cobb, Spalding and many other counties. On the high ridges of North Georgia fruit gets above the frost line, and is thus protected from the late cold snaps. In such localities it is safe from anything but a very hard freeze, which is a rare occurrence after the peach blooms. To protect fruit from cold the Georgia Weather Service, under Director Park Morrill, now forecast official at Washington, organized a system of frost warnings. Bulletins predicting frost or cold waves were sent by telegraph to all stations where there were commercial orchards, and in addition were generally telegraphed to the press of the State. Upon receipt of this information it was possible to protect the fruit by the use of smudges, covering the orchard with smoke and retarding radiation from the ground, while at the same time the temperature was increased above. This method, where persistently tried, has been successful.

Some idea of the profit in peaches in Middle Georgia may be had from the fact that Mr. Rumph sold a crop on the trees in his Marshallville orchard for $60,000. The late Judge John D. Cunningham, who had orchards of about 20,000 trees near Griffin, told the writer that a peach crop one year in five was profitable, as one crop would pay for the orchard and more. At the same time he announced his intention of planting 20,000 more peach trees in Cobb county. This purpose has been carried out by his son, John D. Cunningham, Jr., who has covered the slope of Kennesaw Mountain with an orchard.

Dairying.

The following article, by Col. R. J. Redding, director of the Georgia Experiment Station, may be accepted as thoroughly reliable:

NOTES ON CHEESE MAKING IN GEORGIA.

1. Character and cost of building:

Any cheap outbuilding, or mere shed, will answer all purposes for making cheese. It is only necessary to be dry and comfortable for the operator. But the curing room should be tight and close, yet capable of ventilation. A good 8 by 10 pantry, or storeroom, such as may be found in most well-built farm houses, would answer.

2. Fixtures, machinery, etc.:

A cheese vat, consisting of a wooden box lined with tin, with a small furnace underneath; a press with one or more screws, similar to a cider-press screw; a few tin cheese hoops of different sizes; curd knives, strainers, dipper and a thermometer. The entire outfit for a dairy of twenty-five cows will cost less than $100.

3. The process of cheese making is, briefly, as follows:

The night's milk is kept in a cool place until morning, when it is mixed with the morning's milk and all poured into the cheese vat and heated up to a temperature of 84 degrees. A small quantity of prepared rennet (rennetine) is then added, and the milk is constantly but gently stirred (to prevent the cream from rising) until it commences to thicken. In about forty minutes the milk will become solid; it curdles (you would call it clabber, or sweet curds). When the curd has become pretty firm it is cut into small cubes—about the size and shape of dice—by means of the curd knives, which is done in a few moments. The heat is then increased until the curds show a temperature of 96 to 98 degrees by the thermometer. This heating is to cause the pieces of curd to contract, thereby expelling the whey. The whey is then drained away, and is used to feed pigs, young calves, etc., being fattening food.

The curd is now salted at the rate of one-half ounce of salt to the pound of curd, and the latter is enclosed in a press cloth and put into the cheese hoop and pressed until the whey is all expelled, which will be in about twenty minutes. The cheese is now removed from the press hoop, the press cloth removed, and the permanent cloth "bandage" put on, and then returned to the hoops and press, where it is pressed with the full force of the press and screw and a three-foot lever—the firmer the better.

The cheese usually remains in the press until the next day, or say eighteen hours, when it is marked with date of making and placed on a shelf in the curing room, to be turned over every day and rubbed with the hand. The curing room should be kept at about the temperature of 70 or 75 degrees by opening windows and doors at night and closing up during the day.

The cheese will be ready for use in from three weeks to several months, as may be determined by the maker during the process of making.

4. In the South the months of March, April, May, June, August, September and October are the best cheese-making months, but cheese may be made at any season. Usually cheese is made in spring, summer and fall, and butter in winter, because butter making requires a cool temperature, which cannot be secured in summer without the aid of ice, which is too expensive and inconvenient.

5. How to dispose of milk when not made into cheese:

It is generally more profitable to sell milk than either butter or cheese ; but milk will keep only a few hours, and cannot be sent long distances. Therefore the milk market is easily glutted Butter making is the better way unless a large number of cows are kept and the local market not reliable for milk. Generally cheese making will be found more profitable than either when operating with a good-sized herd.

6. In Georgia nine and one-half pounds of milk are required to make one pound of cured cheese.

7. As before stated, the curds may be manipulated so as to make a long keeping or short keeping cheese—say from three to four weeks to six months may intervene between making and marketing, according to the will of the maker.

When a cheese becomes ripe, or ready for eating, and it is desired to hold it for a better market, it must be kept in a cool room—in summer time in "cold storage."

Transportation.

Georgia has the advantage of fine harbors at Savannah and Brunswick, and South Carolina has two in Charleston and Port Royal. The latter port has been selected by the government for a dry dock. Steamers sail directly from Brunswick and Port Royal to Liverpool and a steady effort is being made to build up direct trade between these ports and European cities. Savannah is rapidly growing in importance as a port. She is the outport for 1,100,000 bales of cotton, or about the quantity raised in Georgia. Brunswick has shipped as high as 200,000 bales. These ports get cotton from Alabama, while some of the North Georgia cotton goes overland to New York and Norfolk.

Atlanta is the natural gateway for the railway system of the South. The great rail lines formerly known as the Richmond and Danville, the Georgia Pacific and the East Tennessee, Virginia and Georgia have been consolidated in the Southern Railway, which will also get the Central system and with it the Georgia Railroad and the Atlanta and West Point Railway, thus controlling seven out of ten lines running into the city. Competing with this giant combination are the Louisville and Nashville and the Seaboard Air Line, both of which are in very strong hands.

The Seaboard Air Line has recently bought the Macon and Northern, giving it access to the center of the State, where it meets the Georgia Southern and Florida, which extends to Palatka, giving a through line for Florida travel from the East and for freight business between Baltimore and the orange region.

Coming into the State from the west is the Macon and Birmingham, not yet complete, but intended to connect with the Kansas City, Fort Scott and Gulf and the Kansas City, Memphis and Birmingham.

Farther south the Savannah, Americus and Montgomery traverses the wiregrass region and connects with the Louisville and Nashville at Montgomery. Still farther down the Plant system crosses the State twice and connects it with the Atlantic Coast Line on the east and with Montgomery via the Alabama Midland on the west.

Thus we have six powerful systems competing for the business of Georgia, with branches interlocking at many points. So elaborate are their ramifications that they are compelled to organize the Southern Railway and Steamship Association to keep from destroying each other. These are:

The Southern Railway, east, west and north.

The Central Railroad, in connection with the Georgia, the Southwestern, and the Atlanta and West Point.

The Louisville and Nashville Railroad, west and north, in connection with the N. C. & St. L. and the Atlanta and West Point.

The Seaboard Air Line, east.

The Savannah, Americus and Montgomery, west.

The Plant System, east and west.

These with a number of minor roads reach every part of the State.

Permeated by these magnificent systems, with 5,100 miles of track for 59,000 square miles of land, it is not surprising that Georgia is well served at reasonable rates in the transportation of freight and passengers. The rates here are in many places lower than the average for like distances because of the part which water routes play in the competition. Two lines of steamships ply between Savannah and New York and Boston, another between Brunswick and New York and a third between Charleston and New York, while recently enlisted lines of English steamships sail from Brunswick and Port Royal for European ports. Water rates between New York and Savannah, Charleston or Brunswick affect the overland rail rates for many miles west of these ports.

The contour of the Atlantic Coast, curving far inward to the west from Cape Hatteras, gives the Georgia ports a geographical advantage which must tell on the development of the railway system of the South, and must eventually build up an immense commerce between these ports and foreign countries. The granary of this continent, with Kansas City or St. Louis as its depot, is 300 miles nearer the Georgia ports than it is to New York. Railway statistics show that the average cost of hauling freight is about two-thirds of a cent per ton per mile, and a saving of 300 miles in distance must mean a saving of two dollars a ton on the haul from the West to the Georgia coast, other conditions being equal. The other conditions are not equal. They favor the Southern route. In this climate car wheels last longer and cost less, lumber and box cars cost less, ties are cheaper and labor is less. With the same volume of business it will cost less to haul freight on Southern railways. As a proof of this, the railways of the South Atlantic States haul freight for less per ton-mile than the roads of more thickly settled sections of the country.

In Virginia and the Carolinas the charge is 81 hundredths of a cent per ton-mile. In Georgia, Alabama, Florida and Mississippi, it is 95 hundredths of a cent. In Illinois, Wisconsin, Iowa and the Dakotas, it is 98 hundredths of a cent.

Local freights in Georgia are regulated by the railroad commission, which prescribes uniform rates for specified distances. The passenger rate is 3 cents a mile and on special occasions it is lower, often a cent a mile. Suburban residents who go into the cities everyday are given rates as low as $5/8$ of a cent per mile.

Manufactures.

The manufactures of the Piedmont States got a great impetus from the Cotton Exposition of 1881. The proximity of raw material with cheap labor and a large home market was not realized by the country before, but in the decade between 1880 and 1890, this region has had the attention of the world. Its wonderful possibilities as the seat of iron and steel industries have been told in enthusiastic terms by such authorities as Sir Lowthian Bell in England and Abram S. Hewitt in this country. As the result, a great impetus was given to all branches of this and other industries in Alabama. In ten years the manufactured products jumped from thirteen to fifty-one millions, and the city of Birmingham sprang up like magic. A whole brood of smaller cities like Anniston, Sheffield and Decatur grew apace and erected immense plants for work in iron and coal. Hundreds of miles of railway were built, and the locomotive's whistle waked echoes in many a wild mountain glen which had hardly known the voice of man.

In the meantime the more varied manufactured products of Georgia and the Carolinas doubled and the number of wage-workers increased in about the same proportion. The profits of manufacture increased for both capital and labor. Raw materials had been enhanced by manipulation only about 50 per cent. in 1880. In 1890 they were worth nearly double after being manufactured. This increase of profit was divided about equally between capital and labor. In Georgia the average wages in manufactories grew from $210 to $309, and in Atlanta they reached $438, in Charleston $422, Savannah $497, and Birmingham $554.

This increase in profit to capital and wages to labor was due to an increasing diversity and refinement of industry. Labor is steadily becoming more efficient and receives higher remuneration.

This gratifying progress of a decade is only a beginning. With immense deposits of coal and iron lying in sight of each other, and with an almost embarrassing variety of minerals, coupled with timber and cotton, it would seem that the Piedmont region should be one of the most important manufacturing districts in the world. Professor Shaler, in his work on "Man and Nature in America," gives a large estimate of the possibilities of industry in the Piedmont region, and every authority in industrial matters, who has seen or studied this country, has pronounced it one of the richest on earth. The rate of progress in ten years gives promise of great development, but after all it is the first round of the ladder. Georgia, with her 68 millions of manufactures, is not in hailing distance of Massachusetts. That little State, with its big population, would starve to death on agriculture; but it sells twelve times as much stuff as Georgia. It takes less cotton than Georgia produces and makes it equal to the cotton of Georgia, Alabama and the Carolinas. Massachusetts has only a fifth more people than Georgia, but she makes of all products more than twelve times as much. One man there turns out as much to sell as a dozen men in Georgia. It is not because men are bigger, or more capable, or more industrious, but simply because Massachusetts has been trained to manufacturing for a century, while up to thirty years ago the people of the South gave almost their entire attention to agriculture. Peculiar conditions made it so, but those conditions have passed away and the best ability of the Piedmont region is turning its attention to manufactures, transportation and commerce. The leading and most sagacious men are preparing for an expansion of trade and industry upon a large scale. Almost every year since 1887 a display of the resources of this region has been made at the Piedmont Exposition at Atlanta, but the ideas and the energies of the people have outgrown that, and they are now preparing for a colossal exposition of the resources and products of all the cotton States, together with those of Mexico and Central and South America. Merchants and manufacturers are already preparing for the exchange of products that will result, and everything points to a tremendous development of trade and industry.

A glance at several industries will show what rapid strides are being made in the Piedmont States. Of the 267 millions of cotton goods made in the United States, only 51 millions are made in the South. Two-thirds of this, or 33½ millions, are made in Georgia, Alabama and the Carolinas. In the last decade this business has doubled in Georgia and quadrupled in the Carolinas. It is no wonder, for some of the Carolina mills have declared 20 per cent. dividends.

The consumption of cotton by Northern mills in 1893 was 1,747,000, about the same as it was ten years ago. In the meantime, Southern mills increased their consumption of cotton from 188,000 to 733,000 bales. Of this amount the mills of Georgia and the Carolinas take 570,000. In twelve years the number of spindles in the South increased from a half million to two millions, and in 1893 143,000 spindles were started and mills for 116,000 more were under construction.

These conditions have been recognized and emphasized of late as never before. Within the past few months several of the largest cotton mill companies of Massachusetts have asked for charter amendments which would allow them to establish new mills in the Piedmont Region of the South. Carolina and Georgia have already received a large influx of New England capital for this purpose, and the investment from that source has reached several millions within a few months. Not less gratifying is the fact that Southern mills, operated by Southern capital, are largely increasing their capacity. The increase from this source is larger than that from New England, but the removal of capital from Massachusetts to Georgia and South Carolina does away with the old idea, so tenaciously held in the East, that climatic conditions for cotton manufacture are not so favorable in the South as in New England. The logic of events has exploded this theory, which long operated like a fetish against investment, and the tide is setting this way as never before.

In the meantime the lumber industry doubled in Georgia and the Carolinas, and naval stores quadrupled in Georgia; the cotton seed oil industry sprang up from nothing to $1,676,000 in Georgia, a million in South Carolina, a half million in North Carolina and a million and a quarter in Alabama. Iron and steel in Alabama jumped from a million and a half to twelve and a half millions, coke from $148,000 to $2,474,000 and lumber from three to nine millions.

These are but a few items. The long list of small industries, which yield the largest profit on the smallest investment, has increased from two to three times as fast as the larger items, showing that the manufactures of this region are taking on that diversity which is the surest guaranty of stability. An important fact for the prospective manufacturer to consider is the amount of capital which must be locked up in material during the process of manufacture and until the finished product is realized upon. In the Piedmont States this is only about two-thirds of the amount required in the country at large. In Georgia it requires only $639 of raw material to the operative; in the United States, $1,098.

In the United States the outlay for material and labor is $1,573 and the profit $421, or 26 per cent; in Georgia labor and material cost $948 and the profit is $283, or 30 per cent. That is to say, two millions of capital will keep at work in the Piedmont region as many operatives as three millions will give employment to in the country at large, and with a little larger per cent. of profit.

Mr. Edward Atkinson has contended that the cotton States were hampered by climatic conditions in the manufacture of cotton above the coarser grades. He was able to convince many for a while, but the present heavy movement of capital from New England to the Piedmont region for investment in cotton mills would lead one to believe that Mr. Atkinson's theory had lost credence. It has a few believers in the Southern mills, but most Southern spinners scout the idea that fine cottons cannot be spun and woven in this climate.

Not long ago, at a banquet tendered to the press associations, then convened in Atlanta, by the management of the Cotton States and International Exposition, Mr. D. A. Tompkins, the distinguished mechanical engineer who organized the Southern Cotton Oil Company, made a statement which will remove the impression that manufactures cannot flourish South as well as North. He said that up to 1810, when slavery began to exert an influence on industrial pursuits, the manufactures of the Southern States exceeded those of the North, but after that, as slavery carried the South into agriculture, the Northern States pushed far ahead. After emancipation an industrial revolution began in the South, and since 1880, the manufacture of cotton and iron in these States has steadily gained on the same industries North. Mr. Tompkins cited the United States census as his authority, and predicted that the Piedmont States would again hold in manufactures the position from which they departed eighty years ago.

WATER POWER.

When coal and wood are exhausted, water will take their place as fuel. This is to be done through electricity. There is enough water power in Georgia to run the railroads, drive the machinery, light the cities and cook the food of many times the present population. A vast number of wheels and spindles are now driven by water power, but when the appliances for transforming this into electric power are so perfected as to come into every-day use, the demand for the power in these streams will be multiplied. When once the transferability of this power is demonstrated it will become a resource of inestimable value to the State of Georgia.

The rivers which furnish the water powers of Georgia are the Chattahoochee, Ocmulgee, Etowah, Yellow, South, Savannah, Tugaloo and minor streams. Thousands of spindles are run by these streams at Augusta, Columbus and points in the interior, but only a small part of the water power of the State is utilized. Within a few miles of almost any large town or city there is water power enough to furnish all its light and power. Full details may be had from the special report on water power in the 10th census.

Minerals of Georgia.

BY PROF. N. P. PRATT.

Outside of the clays and some minor phosphate deposits, the geological formations north of a line drawn through Augusta, Macon and Columbus carry the bulk of the minerals of economic value in Georgia, and practically all these are in the metamorphic, silurian and carboniferous formations.

In the metamorphic we find kaolin, asbestos, corundum, iron pyrites, copper pyrites, mica, all of the gold deposits, magnetic iron ore, specular iron ore, graphite, immense granite quarries and marble deposits, silver bearing galena at Graves Mountain in Columbia county, soapstone and other forms of talc.

In the Silurian formation we find probably the most important deposits of bauxite in America and these overlap into Alabama. The limonite iron ores and the ores of manganese, the limestones, both for furnace fluxes and for building purposes, yellow and red ochre and barytes occur in the Silurian.

The carboniferous formation contains the only deposits of coal in Georgia. They are confined to the northwestern corner of the State, and though not as extensive as those of Alabama, Tennessee or Kentucky, are of great importance. The coal of North Carolina, belonging to a far more recent formation, has no prototype in this State.

In the Red Mountain group, which runs through Northwest Georgia into Alabama, we find the fossiliferous iron ores, which for quantity stand at the head of the iron ores in Alabama. These are the ores which built up the city of Birmingham.

In the Devonian formation, crossing through Northwest Georgia, we find the representative of the recently found phosphatic stratum of Tennessee; but up to date no workable deposits of phosphate have been located on the Georgia side.

In the more recent formations between the metamorphic and the coast, we find clays valuable for various purposes, deposits of marls, and probably a few of the only workable deposits of phosphate that exist. These, so far as present information goes, are confined to Southwest Georgia, near the Florida line.

This brief running sketch refers, not to minerals interesting as scientific curiosities, but to those which mean freight to the railroads, the employment of large capital in their development and labor for thousands of men.

To illustrate: take the asbestos industry, which has just begun in Georgia. Southwest of Clarkesville, a Chicago company hauls by wagon thirty tons a day for a distance of twelve miles. This means work for teams and men, and heavy freight for the railroad. The asbestos is shipped to Chicago and made into indestructible fire brick, besides being used for a variety of other purposes.

The copper belt of Northwest Georgia is a continuation of that which is now being worked for copper so extensively just across the Tennessee border at Ducktown. The ore is low grade and contains only $3\frac{3}{4}$ per cent. of copper, and the operations to be profitable must be on a large scale. One company mines and smelts 125 tons of ore per day and is now preparing to increase its capacity to 250 tons. A neighboring concern nearer the Georgia line has just begun operations on about the same scale as the other.

In the line of pyrites, we have one or two small leads running through Paulding, Douglas and Haralson counties. These mines have lain undeveloped for lack of transportation and because of some uncertainty as to their quantity, etc. In Northeast Georgia, however, there is one of the most important deposits of pyrites in America. The value of this industry to the State can be seen from the fact that the company which owns it is preparing to develop it even though its nearest railroad point is eighteen miles. The consumption of brimstone in the manufacture of sulphuric acid has decreased enormously in the last few years, by reason of the fact that sulphuric acid is made from iron pyrites imported from Spain. Iron pyrites, for the manufacture of sulphuric acid in competition with brimstone, will take the market at any figure the brimstone producer can make, as soon as the demand for the ore can be supplied by the domestic mines. The reason is that pyrites is crude material, blasted out and shipped to the consumer in that form, while brimstone is a manufactured product and has to stand transportation three or four thousand miles besides heavy mining and refining costs, etc.

Georgia has annually paid out perhaps more than half a million dollars for sicilian brimstone used in the manufacture of fertilizers. The sulphuric acid made from pyrites will replace that made from imported brimstone. With the newly discovered Tennessee deposits, the interior districts of Georgia have at hand, with little to pay for freight, the chief materials for sulphuric acid besides phosphate rock. These are the two elements which constitute the bulk of the fertilizers used in Georgia. When it is known that the farmers of the State pay $6,000,000 to $8.000,000 per annum for fertilizers, the importance of this conjunction of raw material will appear.

Sulphuric acid is the basis of all chemical manufactures, and the amount of capital invested in making this acid in England amounts to many millions of pounds sterling. The manufacture of sulphuric acid for chemical fertilizers constitute nine-tenths of the chemical industry of the Southern States.

Georgia has several of the few workable deposits of manganese in this country, the next in importance being in Arkansas. Georgia has also one of two localities in the United States producing corundum in commercial quantities. The other is in North Carolina. That State carries about all the varieties of the valuable minerals which Georgia carries, except perhaps bauxite and a few others.

Northwest Georgia has numerous fine developments of iron ores, the combination of limonite and fossiliferous ores making a high metal easily smelted.

There are furnaces at Rome, Cedartown, Hermitage, Etna and near points in Alabama. The manganese mined is shipped to Pittsburg, where it is extensively used by the Carnegie Company.

The gold mines of Georgia were until recently worked by old hydraulic processes. Now the old Franklin mines in Cherokee county have a chlorination plant and it is operated with great success and profit. Before the discovery of gold in California the mines of Georgia were considered among the most important in the United States, and a branch of the United States mint was located at Dahlonega. Of late there is renewed interest in our gold fields and new plants are being put in to mine the ores extensively according to modern processes.

The development of the marble industry within the past ten years has been rapid, and it is to-day one of the most important industries in the State, with several millions of capital invested. The principal works are at Marietta, the quarries being at other points on the Marietta and North Georgia Railroad.

Georgia was the pioneer of the iron industry in the South. This fact is attested by twelve old rock furnace stacks still standing in Bartow county, where also one of the first rolling mills in the Southern States was situated.

Wealth, Debt and Taxation.

In wealth Georgia reached in 1888 the point from which she departed in 1861. Barring slave property, she returned as much to the tax-gatherer as she had twenty-seven years before. Through the devastation of war and the spoliation of the carpet-bag era she had lost more than half her wealth, besides losing in men a large part of the force which was to rebuild. A child born in time to hear the last thunders of war was not mature, before the scarred hilltops were smiling with plenty. Kennesaw Mountain, where ten thousand men were hurled to death, is now one vast orchard, where literally their swords have been beaten into ploughshares and their spears into pruning hooks. From two hundred millions in 1870 the tax return had grown to three hundred and fifty-seven millions in 1888, and four hundred and fifty-two millions in 1893. During the last five years before the panic Georgia added one hundred millions to her wealth and a hundred and fifty thousand to her population. Railroads that were streaks of rust, covering only fourteen hundred miles at the end of the war, now extend over five thousand miles, with steel rails, ballasted track and iron bridges.

With all this increase in wealth, the public and private indebtedness is trifling in comparison with that of other states. Georgia's Railroad property will pay the State debt, for the rental of the State Road is fifty thousand dollars more than the interest on the State bonds; the counties and cities owe little, and the people owe less per capita than those of any other state except Arkansas. It is $15 a head in Georgia and $13 in Arkansas, $26 in Alabama and $23 in Tennessee, against $51 in Indiana, $100 in Illinois, $104 in Iowa, $170 in Kansas, $152 in Minnesota and $72 in Wisconsin. If it is true that debts are harder to pay as commodities depreciate, Georgia and her sister states are freer from this financial thralldom than any other portion of the Union. While Georgia, Tennessee and Florida land is mortgaged for only seven or eight per cent. of its value, that of Kansas is bound for 27 per cent., Minnesota for 21 per cent. and Iowa for 17 per cent. The Eastern States are mortgaged from 18 to 30 per cent., but mostly on city property, which has a steady income, depending less on the value of commodities than the agricultural lands of the West and South.

State Treasurer R. U. Hardeman was requested to give a statement of Georgia's finances and has done so concisely but comprehensively in the letter which appears below :

ATLANTA, September, 24, 1894.

The rate of taxation for general purposes is 99-100 of a mill, which is, I believe, the lowest in the Union. Including the amounts raised by the State for pensions and for schools, which are paid for by local taxation in some states, the State tax is 4.37 mills. For specific purposes, such as schools and pensions, it is as follows:

For schools, 2.24 mills.

For pensions of confederate soldiers and widows of soldiers, 1.08 mills.

The State of Georgia appropriates $1,253,000 for schools, all of which is included in the above rate of 2.24 mills, though only about half of it, $688,000, comes from direct taxation. About $200,000 comes from the poll tax, $210,000 from half the rental of the W. & A. Railroad, and the remainder from specific taxes on liquor dealers, circuses, etc.

The State debt is $8,149,500, on which the interest is $368,835, payable in January and July. Against this the State has assets as follows:

The W. & A. Railroad, which is leased for 29 years from January 1st, 1891, to the Nashville, Chattanooga and

St. Louis Railway Company at a rental of $420,000 per annum. Upon this income the property should be worth, on a five per cent. valuation, $8,400,000.

The State owns 186 shares of Georgia Railroad and Banking Company stock of the par value of $18,600, but worth in the market 148, or $27,528. Also $10,000 of Southern Atlantic Telegraph Company stock, endorsed by the Western Union Telegraph Company and worth par.

The State also owns several public buildings of which the capitol cost $1,000,000. This building is remarkable not only because it is one of the finest and most imposing edifices in America, but because it was built by direct taxation within the appropriation. When it was completed the Capitol Commissioners returned to the treasury $196 of the original appropriation.

As State Treasurer it is my duty to visit and inspect once a year all the banks chartered under the laws of Georgia. There are 108 such institutions, with a capital of $10,324,530 and a surplus of $1,697,000. During the panic of 1893 there were but two failures among these institutions. In both cases the depositors will be paid in full.

One of the most important features of finance in Georgia is the facility for collection and the security offered for money at the rate of 8 per cent., which is the legal contract rate of the State. R. U. HARDEMAN,
Treasurer of Georgia.

COUNTY TAXATION.

The county tax for local purposes goes to make a part of the burden of government. The rate varies somewhat in different counties, but the average of State and county taxation combined is about 1 per cent. Railroads, except a few of the earlier ones, which are exempt by charter, have to pay State and county tax, and from this source about $200,000 of the State's revenue arises. About the same amount is paid to the counties by railroads.

The Constitution of the State prohibits counties or cities from incurring debt in excess of 7 per cent. upon the value of their taxable property. This has been found a salutary check upon extravagance in the administration of municipal and county governments.

Education in Georgia.

BY HON. S. D. BRADWELL, EX-STATE SCHOOL COMMISSIONER.

The Common School System.—Georgia has made great advancement in the line of popular education. The system is yet in its infancy, having been in existence less than a quarter of a century. Under the old system the benefit could only be obtained by those who had means and education was therefore confined to the few.

In consequence of events following the war a change in that old system became absolutely necessary. An education, from being a luxury, was regarded as a necessity.

At first a small sum of less than $200,000 was appropriated for common school purposes, but the fund has grown until now it is beyond a million and a quarter each year. From two months, which was the limit of the free schools in the State at the beginning in 1871, the term has been extended gradually to five months, which period is obligatory upon the school officers. In the towns, by means of increased taxation authorized by the local system, schools continue eight to ten months each year and are free to all.

The most perceptible improvement is in the country schools. The old-time teacher, whose information was limited to the three R's, has disappeared, and live, progressive teachers have taken his place. In all little communities and villages the five months' schools made free by State appropriation are supplemented by voluntary aid on the part of the patrons, and there are very few localities where there are 40 or 50 children within reach of the school room which cannot by means of these additional voluntary contributions secure at least 8 months tuition. Of course, in some sparsely settled localities and among the very poorest class of our tenantry, the five months' school is the only means of education. These schools are taught by teachers who during the other seven months of the year are engaged in making a crop by which they supplement the little sum received from the State for their five months' work.

Each year sees a very great improvement on the part of the teachers. Heretofore the State has done but little for them in the way of normal instruction, but for three years they have been brought together for a week at a time at stated intervals to obtain instruction in the principles, plans and methods of teaching. This plan bears good fruit. The teachers, drawn closer together, become more impressed with the responsibility of their work and more alive to the interests of the State and of the children. Greater uniformity and proficiency in school work are noticeable each session. Examinations are more thorough and the teachers evince greater desire to rise higher in the calling. The great tendency of the institute work has been to elevate teaching into a profession, and the policy of the State will continue in this direction until the teacher is placed upon the same plane occupied by other public servants or by men and women in professional life.

Higher Education.—The State University is each year sending forth scores of active, energetic, cultured young men, who are making their mark in all the avocations of life. Many of them choose the profession of teaching and become the life of the school system.

The number annually enrolled in the University at Athens generally exceeds 250, and a still greater number are in the branch colleges at other points. With a larger fund the good work done by the University would be appreciated in every town and village of Georgia.

As a branch of the State University, the Agricultural College at Athens offers ample facilities for young men who desire to prepare themselves thoroughly for the work of agriculture, horticulture or dairying.

High praise is due the Georgia Institute of Technology at Atlanta, which is the largest branch of the State University. It is equipped with a machine shop modeled after that at the Worcester School of Technology, which is considered the best in the land Accompanying it is the academic building with a fine equipment of chemical and physical apparatus. This institution, in addition to a liberal education, gives a thorough training in all the departments of handicraft; and that the work in this institution is of a high character is demonstrated by the fact that the young men who complete the course have no trouble in securing fine positions as machinists, electricians, contractors, etc., in all sections of the country.

The higher institutions of learning which are directly under the patronage of the State University, generally known as branch colleges, such as the School of Technology at Atlanta, the Girls' Normal and Industrial School at Milledgeville, and the North Georgia Agricultural College at Dahlonega, have accomplished great good in the way of secondary higher education.

Too much cannot be said in praise of the institution for the girls at Milledgeville. Its establishment was an act of tardy justice to the girls, who had not been cared for by the State beyond the common schools. After leaving the grammar school the girl was dismissed from the educational care of the State and thrown upon her own responsibility. The institution at Milledgeville comes in as a college for young ladies, giving collegiate advantages, as well as special training in normal work and in many of the industrial arts. The branch college at Dahlonega is also open to both sexes, and girls and boys are in the same classes, pursuing the same branches of study.

It would not be amiss, in this connection, to speak of the good work done by the colored branch of the State University. Georgia has not been remiss in her efforts to give the negro the benefits of higher education. This is an institution located at Savannah as a branch of the university, well equipped and manned entirely by negro teachers. It is supported by State funds raised by taxation. The annual appropriation is $14,000.

As an evidence of the growth of the common school system, one need look only at the number who are receiving elementary instruction from the State and the State alone. At the organization of the system in 1871 the enrollment was 49,578, of which 42,914 were white and 6,664 colored. In 1893 the total enrollment was 425,000, of which 260,000 were white and 165,000 were colored. In 1871 only about one-fourth the children of school age were enrolled; now two-thirds are on the rolls, and it is safe to predict that 1894 will show a large gain over 1893. In 1871 the entire school fund, including poll tax, did not much exceed a quarter of a million; now it is about $1,300,000, having been multiplied nearly five times in twenty-three years. This shows that the public school system is growing, not like a mushroom, but with a healthy, substantial growth. The growth of years is not likely to be destroyed or seriously impaired by the first storm of adverse agitation or demagogical outcry. Popular education has found its way to the hearts of the people of Georgia, and all opposition to the education of the children, so far as preparing them for the active duties of citizenship goes, has ceased.

The fund for the support of common schools is derived from certain specific taxes which, of course, are paid by the consumer, the poll tax and the direct property tax. This year the direct tax is $600,000, the specific taxes amount to about $500,000, and the poll tax about $200,000, making the entire school fund about $1,300,000. To realize the amount of direct tax from property, a levy of $1.44 on the thousand has been made for the year 1894, so that the educational tax in Georgia can be put down as about $1.44 on each $1,000 worth of property. If the specific taxes were paid directly into the treasury and the entire school fund had to be raised by direct taxation, it would require a levy of only $2.30 on the $1,000. The school tax in Georgia is, therefore, not burdensome, and when we take into consideration that there are 605,000 children who are to be recipients of the benefits of the public school fund, a great work is being accomplished by this small tax. Additional local taxes are levied for the support of local institutions. The general fund, however, suffices for five months' schools everywhere.

It is clear that schools which are in operation for eight months must be more effective, by reason of more thorough, accurate and better work on the part of the teachers— teachers who are prepared for the work, who make it their only business— than those schools which are limited to 100 days in the year, where the children are often taken out of school to work on the farm, and where the term has to be accommodated to the wants of an agricultural community, frequently dividing the term of five months into fifty days in the early spring and fifty days in the late fall; but there is improvement on this line where the communities have a population thick enough to keep up permanent schools.

Some of the very best schools in Georgia are to be found in the smaller towns and villages, where experienced teachers have made their impress by long continued work in the same school room. I taught school twenty years in one house which I owned in a small community where the local patronage is not more than twenty, and built up in that way a large school, where ten to fifteen counties were represented. Without being egotistical I could say that it was my school. I made an impress which would have been impossible had I been one year in one place and the next in another.

Such schools were common in many of the counties before the war, and many of our ablest statesmen received there the first and strongest impetus of their intellectual life. Such schools are still scattered through the country and they are strengthened mightily by the help which they get from their *pro rata* of the common school fund. Their main support is from the State, but this is supplemented often by local aid, either voluntry or by local taxation.

While the common school fund is limited to the elementary branches, yet by a very generous ruling of the department, where a child devotes as much as half his time to the common school branches, he is classed as a common school pupil, although the other half of his time may be devoted to higher branches. By this classification such pupils are entitled to their *pro rata* of the common school fund. Then by a combination with philanthropic associations and chartered organizations the same thing is effected on the idea that they have a common school department, devoting most of their time to these branches.

In any community where there are children enough to constitute a school they can obtain recognition, be located and with a licensed teacher obtain their share of the public school fund from the State.

Labor.

At the close of the civil war, the labor system of the South had to be reorganized. The old relation of master and slave had to be changed to that of capital and labor. The former system had the tendency of feudalism to build up great agricultural estates. The new arrangement necessitated a division of the plantations into farms, with culture upon the intensive plan.

The census shows this very clearly. In the last thirty years there has been a steady and rapid decrease in the size of farms. Here are the figures:

ACRES TO THE FARM.

	1860.	1870.	1880.	1890.
Alabama	346	222	139	126
Georgia	430	338	188	147
South Carolina	488	233	143	115
North Carolina	316	212	142	127

One plantation of 1860 makes three or four farms of 1890.

The change in tillage methods is accurately represented in these figures, but the change in ownership is not so great as they indicate, for it appears that the census classifies rented land as a separate farm, though several such leases may be made on one plantation owned by one man. In 1880, 64 per cent. of the farms in the South Atlantic States was cultivated by owners. In 1890 it was 61 per cent. In Georgia the till~ by owners fell from 55 to 46 per cent. This change is due to the fact that owners of the large plantations are getting in the habit of renting a part of their land and tilling a smaller acreage themselves. Thus, a man with 300 acres will often rent 100, and make as much on the remainder, by thorough tillage, as he used to make on the whole. The tenant, meantime, is thrown on his own responsibility, and cultivates the other part better. The result is a gain, both to the owner and to the laborer, who has become a tenant. It is this process more than actual change of ownership, which is reducing the average size of farms so rapidly in the South. With negro labor, it is perhaps the best system that could be devised, but with an influx of white labor it would readily give way to small proprietorship, for the farmer realizes that he has surplus land, and is ambitious to make better crops on smaller acreage, provided he can sell enough surplus land to pay his debts.

The tendency is toward a diffusion of wealth among the rural population. There are fewer dignitaries and more laborers, fewer plantations and more farms. Free labor costs little more than slave labor. Before the war the negro got his board and clothes, shelter and medical attention. In the past thirty years he got that and fourteen millions more. This difference is not a dollar per annum for the individual. Above that, however, besides a little spending money, the negro got schooling for his children at his own or the State's expense. Of 290,000 colored children of school age in Georgia, 165,000 are enrolled this year. Fifty-seven per cent. avail themselves of the privilege in one year, but 73 per cent. have escaped illiteracy. With the rapid progress in extending the school system, the number of those who cannot read and write will be very small a few years hence.

Some thinking men have contended that schooling does not make the negro a better laborer, but there can be no question that it will improve him if it is used as a basis for technical training, such as the State has inaugurated for colored youth at Savannah.

A persistent movement of the negro population toward the cities has been disclosed by the United States census.

It is even more noticeable in the school census recently completed by the State. In five years the negroes increased 6 per cent. in the country and 17 in the city. This is true of the white population also, but in the negro's case this movement of population is fraught with special consequences of a disastrous nature. With comparative health in the country, he dies twice as fast as the white man does in the city. The reason is that he occupies largely the slums of Southern cities, and inexorable sanitary laws inflict their fearful penalty upon him. It is because of this movement that the scale of increase has turned in favor of the white man within the past decade. The census shows that in the Piedmont region the whites increased 25 per cent. while the negro grew 13 per cent.

There is in the minds of some a prejudice against colored labor, but the negro has cleared and tilled too much land, built too many dwellings and built too many railroads to be called a poor laborer. With him, as with others, efficiency depends upon training. It is perhaps not surprising that when, after being under the training of intelligent masters, the race was suddenly left to the guidance of ignorant and illiterate parents, many of the younger ones degenerated and became vagrants. But the mass of the race, especially in the rural districts, is yet docile and willing to work if properly trained while young.

But if the negro leaves the fields, it is, as a rule, never to return. White men take his place, and with better training and higher intelligence, they build up a variety and a character of agriculture to which the negro has never aspired. When a white boy leaves the farm and comes to town, he takes great risk; but when a negro makes that venture he courts poverty, disease and perhaps death.

One especially encouraging fact about the negro race is that it is becoming homogeneous. Mr. Charles A. Dana, the distinguished editor of the New York *Sun*, came South three years ago, after an absence of thirty years, and stopped two days at Atlanta. In an interview he pointed out to the writer, as the most noticeable fact which came under his observation, that the negro was getting blacker, and therefore a better and stronger race. It was less contaminated by an illegitimate mixture of white blood. Thirty years before, he had been astonished at the number of light mulattoes; now their absence was noticeable. Mr. Dana's observation is true, and the fact is one of tremendous import. There are two cardinal points upon which the progress of any race will turn: these are virtue in the women and political integrity among the men. With Mr. Dana's testimony on the first point, what may be said for the second? Therein lies the solution of the negro problem.

The negro vote is yet purchasable to some extent. This is the principal bar to progress in the race. Anything that would remove him further from the influence of that poison which stunts his life would be his salvation. This result is being reached by a natural process. The ratio of increase is now against the negro, and if it continues so, he will eventually be in a minority too small to hold the balance of power, and therefore too small to buy in elections. When that happens, the principal, and almost the only cause of irritation and estrangement between the two races will have been removed. All things come to him who waits, and so time will lift the negro out of this political slough. That being true, his future in the industrial world becomes broader and brighter.

But the negro does not monopolize the labor, even the hard labor of this region. He is, by numbers, less than half of it. The Georgia Institute of Technology, like the Alabama Polytechnic Institute, is a movement toward the greater efficiency of white labor. It is a declaration by the State that the best that science or technical skill can do for labor is not too good for it. The young men who go out from these institutes make anything from a hoe handle to an electric motor. The writer has used a motor made by one of them, and has seen hundreds of looms fitted with gearing in the Georgia Institute shop. There are several hundreds of these boys in the polytechnic schools of Georgia and Alabama, and the presence of their graduates is beginning to be felt in all kinds of industry. They hold lucrative positions, not only here, but in other States, from Pennsylvania to Mexico.

For the great mass of labor in Georgia, the most significant fact to recite is that it shows the effect of diffused intelligence, following the extension of the public school system. More reading, better posted men, better farming and better work of all kinds is the tendency. An important result of more reading and thinking among the farmers is that they are getting out of debt and improving their methods of tilling the soil. Less cotton, more grain, grass and fruits, and more profit.

The material of which the white race in Georgia and the Piedmont States is composed came almost exclusively from the British isles. The Huguenots of South Carolina also form a valuable element.

The efficiency of both the white and colored labor in agriculture has never been seriously questioned, but there has been some contention that the Georgia cracker did not make a good mill operative. This contention has come mainly from New England spinners, and a stout contradiction comes from the same quarter. Mr. Joel Smith, superintendent of the King Mill at Augusta, Ga., is a native of New England, trained up under the Slaters. He told the writer in an interview in 1890 that there was no truth in the above assertion, and that the Georgia cracker, with good training, made an excellent operative in cotton mills.

Markets.

There is a topography in prices ascending from West to East. As farm products travel toward the great cities or the Atlantic ports, freight is added to the price, and as they are farther removed from the great granary of the continent and approach nearer to the mass of consumers, the demand grows larger and steadier. England being the center of the world's market for breadstuffs, the price is calculated from the longitude of the ports, with intermediate points in proportion. This effect is heightened by local variations of supply and demand. All these causes combined give the products of the Piedmont region higher prices than most other sections enjoy.

This topography in prices has another aspect. Manufactured and imported goods are higher as they go west. Starting from the ports or the factories, they bear a heavier burden of freight with every degree of west longitude. The farmer in the Piedmont region pays less for goods and receives more for his products than farmers on the western plains. This may partly explain the fact that the mortgage debt of the Piedmont region is only one-fifth to one-tenth as much per capita as it is in the west.

The report of the Secretary of Agriculture shows that the staple crops of grain in the Piedmont region are consumed almost entirely at home. Over 90 per cent. of the corn and wheat crops of 1892 was consumed in the counties where it was grown. As a result, the prices received were not only better than those received in sections exporting a large part of their grain, but were less reduced by the cost of transportation. Of the corn crop of 1892 in Georgia, 95 per cent. was consumed in the counties where it grew; in South Carolina 96 per cent., in North Carolina 93 per cent. and in Alabama 94 per cent. Contrast this with the proportions so consumed in Western States. In Illinois it was 77 per cent., in Indiana 78, in Iowa 81, Kansas 78, Nebraska 58 and California 75. The Secretary of Agriculture remarks upon the variation of prices with localities: "The highest returns are from the New England and mountain regions, where the production is not sufficient for local use, and the lowest naturally from the States which supply commercial corn." Thus it is that while corn was selling for 31 cents in Kansas, 36 cents in Illinois, 40 cents in Indiana, 28 cents in Nebraska, and 45 cents in Texas, it brought 60 cents in Georgia, 57 cents in South Carolina and 52 cents in Alabama. This is an important fact when it is remembered that the corn crop of Georgia is 32,000,000 bushels, that of Alabama is 30,000,000 bushels, and that of North Carolina is 25,000,000 bushels, with a progressive increase of acreage from year to year. As the expansion of the cotton acreage increases on the black lands of Texas and the Mississippi valley, and the price is depressed in the world's market because of a steadily increasing supply, the farmers of Georgia, Alabama, South Carolina and the Piedmont States are turning their attention more and more to grain and the grasses. With the heavy demand for live stock, for which these States have to spend several millions each every year, the demand for corn is likely to increase as fast as the supply, and for years to come this grain promises to be a remunerative crop in the Piedmont region.

The same difference in prices holds good in wheat, and for the same reasons. The wheat crop of 1892 brought 61 cents in Minnesota, Wisconsin and Illinois, and 50 cents in Nebraska and South Dakota, while in North Carolina and Georgia it brought 90 cents. The North Carolina crop of 5,000,000 bushels sold for $4,530,356, according to the report of the Agricultural Department at Washington. The wheat crop of Georgia for that year was 1,474,000 bushels, which brought $1,326,938. This grain is confined to the northern half of the State, forming a part of the Piedmont region. Here the wheat area is extending every year. It is quite likely that the crop of 1894 will be shown by the forthcoming report to be more than 3,000,000 bushels.

Likewise in the price of oats, the Piedmont States enjoy a great advantage. In 1892 the crop in Georgia was 6,090,000 bushels, worth $3,166,673; in North Carolina 5,332,000 bushels, worth $2,399,515; in South Carolina 3,682,000, worth $1,914,708, and in Alabama 3,721,000, worth $1,897,742. The average was about 50 cents a bushel. In Indiana, Illinois, Wisconsin, Minnesota and Iowa it was about 30 cents a bushel.

The average price of horses in January, 1893, was $81 in Georgia, $86 in South Carolina, $77 in North Carolina and $68 in Alabama. In Missouri it was $51, in Kansas $55, in Nebraska 57, South Dakota $63, Iowa $61 and Illinois $65. This winter a car load of horses were sold for a dollar a head in the far west.

Timber.

The timber wealth of the Southern States is one of their greatest resources. The belt of long leaf pine begins in North Carolina and follows the coast plain as far as Texas, extending across seven States and covering about 150,000 square miles. This wonderful tree is almost like cotton in the variety and value of its products. First it is tapped for turpentine, thus yielding in Georgia alone an annual product of five or six millions in naval stores. After the timber has been drained of sap, its tensile strength, according to government tests, remains equal to that of the virgin growth.

The extent of this pine timber has never been accurately measured by the census, but a careful estimate made of the pine belt in Georgia, based on returns from eighty counties, shows that there is not less than forty billion feet standing in the forests of this State. This, at $10 a thousand feet for all classes of lumber, which is a moderate valuation, would make a resource worth four hundred millions. By the present hap-hazard system the sawmills of Georgia have turned out ten million dollars' worth of lumber in a year. If the same systematic and scientific care which is the rule in Europe were taken of the forests of the Southern States, they would yield an annual revenue second only to that of the cotton crop. It is estimated that, with good husbandry, the pine trees of Georgia would yield a yearly product of thirty millions in lumber, without reducing the forests, and that naval stores to the amount of at least ten millions could be added, making a total product of forty millions, a sum fully one-third larger than the present value of Georgia's cotton crop. If the whole long leaf pine belt, from North Carolina to Texas, were treated in the same way, the lumber and naval stores product of these seven States would amount to more than two hundred millions.

The Secretary of the Georgia Sawmill Association, speaking of the importance of the long leaf pine, says: "It is worth as much, tree for tree, as walnut."

In addition to its other uses, the long leaf pine furnishes a straw out of which a factory in North Carolina makes matting and excelsior, and the same concern at one time put on the market a species of bagging made of pine straw for the covering of cotton bales.

The hardwood timber of the Piedmont region is abundant and of superior quality. Hickory and white-oak are particularly valuable, and both are in good supply. The manufacturers of furniture and agricultural implements use large quantities of oak, and the carriage and wagon factories are great consumers of hickory. There is also a considerable supply of ash, maple and beach. In the swamps of the southern part of the State cypress is very abundart, and from it shingles of a very durable character are made.

The export trade in lumber had grown to be a large item before it was checked by the late depression. Georgia pine was shipped through Brunswick, Savannah and Darien to Spain, England and South America. Trade fell off when the crash in the Argentine Republic came, but of late that business is springing up again.

Considering their value, the timber lands of the South have been selling for a song. Thousands of square miles, sold for one or two dollars an acre, have yielded from four to ten times that much in lumber and naval stores. Formerly it was supposed that these pine lands were unfit for culture, but of late they have been made to produce immense crops of corn, potatoes and sea island cotton—a species which brings three times as much as the ordinary staple.

The same lands produce almost the entire watermelon crop of Georgia, which is estimated to be worth more than a million dollars.

Building Stones and Timber Resources

Mr. Charles Morton Strahan, Professor of Civil Engineering at the University of Georgia, has on request, kindly furnished the following article on the building stones and timber resources of this State:

A line running from Columbus to Augusta divides the State in two parts entirely distinct in geologic character and physical outline. Northern Georgia lies at a high elevation above the sea level, is traversed in a southwesterly direction by the Blue Ridge mountains; is everywhere hilly and broken; is covered with a thick forest of oak, short-leaf pine, hickory, ash, and other broad-leaved trees; and is underlaid by metamorphic and crystaline rocks, including granites, marbles and slate, which outcrop along the hills in many places favorable to quarrying.

Southern Georgia, on the contrary, is comparatively flat, is underlaid by the more recent geologic rocks with few outcrops, but is covered by a very dense forest of yellow pine, cypress and oak.

The value of the long-leaf or yellow pine as a timber tree has long been known, and a large amount of capital is invested in pine lands and sawmills located in that belt of territory between the Savannah, Americus and Montgomery Railroad and the southern boundary of the State. The annual cut in 1880 was nearly 300,000,000 feet B. M., and the census estimate of standing pine was nearly 17,000,000,000 feet B. M. This was only an estimate, and is, by well-informed parties, considered very much below the fact. This does not include the heavy growth of cypress which is found in the numberless swamps of South Georgia, nor the large amount of white oak, ash and poplar which are associated with the pine and cypress.

The yellow pine forest has a further value from the large yield of rosin, given by the growing tree. For three years before the trees are cut for sawing they are boxed for the rosin, many thousand barrels of which are annually shipped from South Georgia ports. Yellow pine lumber stands unrivalled for straightness of grain, combined with ease of working, great durability and a strength equal to that of oak. Large bodies of these timber lands still exist untouched by the axe, and can be purchased at prices ranging from $1.50 to $5.00 per acre. The numerous railroads and water courses that traverse the pine lands render transportation easy and cheap.

NORTH GEORGIA.—The timber interests of North Georgia are concerned more especially with the hard-wood trees and with pine lumber made from the short-leaf pine. In 1880, twenty-eight million feet, B. M., of short-leaf pine lumber was cut in Georgia, and perhaps an equal amount of oak. The forests of North Georgia contain not less than fifty varieties of valuable timber trees growing to large sizes, and, according to the census of 1880, with an average density of from 20 to 50 cords per acre. The hard woods of this section are especially suited for the manufacture of agricultural implements, furniture, and wooden utensils of all kinds. Timber lands ranging in price from $1.00 to $25.00 per acre, according to situation.

The inexhaustible deposits of valuable building stones that exist in North Georgia are but little known and only partially developed. The granites are found in the section east of the Blue Ridge, while the marbles and slates are confined to the valleys on the western slope.

GRANITES.—The largest quarries in the state are located near Atlanta on the slopes and in the vicinity of Stone Mountain. This immense mass of granite rock rises above the adjacent country to a height of several hundred feet, and covers a base of several miles in diameter. It forms the centre of a granite section in which many valuable out-crops occur. The quality of stone furnished from this section varies with the quarry. The Stone Mountain granite is more strictly a gneiss rock showing a good deal of mica, and splits readily along certain lines of cleavage. It is grayish white in color, and does not take a high polish. Its principal use has been for Belgian block pavement, and for this purpose it is unexcelled. When used in ornamental masonary it is subject to stain. The quarries at Lithonia yield a Muscovite granite, which bears the strong endorsement of the U. S. Geological Survey and the U. S. Navy Yard. Tests by these parties show a very high breaking strength, almost no porosity, freedom from iron stains, and therefore a stone of great durability and structural value.

The town of Lexington, in Oglethorpe County, is the centre of another territory in which a granite of the very finest quality is found. Lexington granite is a true granite, of close, even texture, bluish-gray in color, absorbs moisture to a very minute amount, and fails to crush under 20,000 lbs. to the square inch. It resembles very closely the celebrated Quincy granite of Massachusetts. It is more difficult to quarry than the Stone Mountain granite, and works harder under the hammer. It is entirely free from iron stains, even after long exposure, and takes a very high polish.

Granite of very good quality is found in the section around Griffin and Newnan, and is quarried in limited quantities.

MARBLES.—The best marble deposits of the State are found in the Long Swamp Valley, Pickens County, and are reached by the Marietta and North Georgia Railroad. This marble is highly crystalline, 10,000 pounds crushing strength, .06 per cent. absorbtion, and does not stain from weathering. It has the highest endorsement from experts, while its beauty and durability have been established by actual use. Three quarries are at work turning out three varieties of marble, white, light pink, and banded black and white. These marbles justly rank among the best and most beautiful building stones in America.

SLATE.—A fine deposit of slate has given rise to a quarry at Rockmart, in Polk County, near Cedartown. The quarry is small but the output is of excellent quality, valued at $4.50 per cubic foot.

The last few years have witnessed a new interest in the development of the quarries of North Georgia. The quality of their outputs has won the confidence of builders and architects, and the demand is rapidly increasing.

Alabama.

Although the scope of this hand-book includes the Piedmont region, and Alabama has been referred to in almost every chapter, it is worth while to devote a few pages especially to a State whose resources are so great.

In the production of iron and coal Alabama leads the South, and has already thrown down the gauntlet to Pennsylvania and Ohio. Nowhere on earth is there such conjunction of coal, iron and limestone as in Alabama. From the crest of Red Mountain range, where the iron ore is twenty-two feet thick, you can look across Limestone valley and see the smoke of the coke ovens at the coal mines.

In the Birmingham region, which is nearly coextensive with Jefferson county, there are thirty iron furnaces and a whole brood of industries of the family of iron. The growth of that city was one of the most rapid on record, and its culmination in 1887 caused such a fever of excitement as few communities have experienced, from commercial or industrial causes, since the days of John Law and the South Sea bubble. The difference is that this was no bubble, and the people who went crazy about Birmingham real estate saw before them in actual and vigorous operation great plants whose daily output was prodigious. In one place four iron furnaces, covering, with all their appurtenances only an acre or two, used 500 cars every day to bring in the ore and coal and carry out the iron.

With such a growth as this it is no wonder that railroad tonnage grew amazingly in Alabama, and the output of manufactures increased from thirteen millions to more than fifty!

But it was not in iron alone that Alabama developed. There was an enormous expansion of the lumber industry, and scores of large mills were built and put in operation. While the output of the mills in Southern Georgia was largely exported, that of Alabama went almost entirely to domestic markets. As the forests of Michigan were thinned and lumber from that source advanced in price, the Southern pine came into request in the markets of the Middle States, particularly in Cincinnati, which was a distributing point for this lumber. At the same time a very large demand for yellow pine for freight cars and bridge timber sprang up among the railroads.

Alabama has been distinguished for her progressive spirit, not only in the development of her mineral and timber resources, but in the encouragement of education of a high grade. The University of Alabama does good work, and the practical equipment given in the polytechnic school at Auburn is fully abreast of the age. There the scientific education is of a high character, and the technical training stands the test of actual work in mechanical engineering and in the construction of machines.

The State government is a progressive one, and for some years the Agricultural Department has accompanied its work for better culture of the soil with an active campaign for immigration. This is done upon the idea that a sale of some of the surplus land to energetic Western farmers would lead to better culture and would be a benefit to all concerned. Carloads of Alabama products have been taken through the Western and Middle States and immense quantities of printed matter have been distributed. By these means and others, a considerable number of good settlers has been added to the agricultural population.

Montgomery, the capital, is one of the most solid and in some ways one of the most enterprising cities in the

South. It was Montgomery capital which built Birmingham. The nestor of that enterprise, Josiah Morris, lived at the capital till he died. Its people are noted for their excellent schools and for their culture. In this connection it should be stated that the public men of Alabama take high rank in the National Congress. Senator Morgan has long been recognized as one of the leaders of the United States Senate, and his position at the head of the foreign affairs committee gives him a reputation beyond the sea, and this has been increased by his part in the deliberations of the Behring Sea Commission.

THE NICARAGUA CANAL.

Senator Morgan's patriotic and statesmanlike efforts for the construction of the Nicaragua canal commend him, not only to the people of Alabama, but to all the Southern States and to the entire country. As both political parties are committed to this great work, it is considered assured, and when it comes, Alabama's industries will have a better and broader market than those of any manufacturing region in the world. It has been predicted that this State will be the seat of the greatest development of the iron and steel industries on the globe, and the opening of a waterway between the Atlantic and the Pacific will tend greatly to hasten the coming of that era.

Mobile, once an important port, is destined again to occupy a commanding position in the event of the opening of the Nicaragua canal. It is still a seat of culture and considerable business, but its future holds promise of real commercial greatness.

Alabama has a number of smaller towns of solidity and promise. Among these are Selma, Anniston and Sheffield. Selma is a strong commercial town in the cotton region, while Anniston and Sheffield are manufacturing towns, based on iron and its various products. Anniston has also a large and prosperous cotton mill, whose products have been exported to China for a number of years. This model city has also a large plant for car building, operated by the United States Rolling Stock Company.

SOILS.

The soils of North Alabama are very similar to those of North Georgia, though mostly differing from the metamorphic formation described by Professor White. They are more like the red soils of Northwest Georgia, where the veins of red ore and limestone are continued. The red lands of Alabama produce well, especially in the valleys and on river and creek bottoms, but any of the red lands may be made very productive by the successive use of leguminous plants and judicious fertilization. The highest hilltops on these red lands are above the frost line and give admirable sites for orchards.

The lower part of the State, known as the black belt, is very rich and produces immense crops of cotton, corn, small grain and grasses.

There is in Alabama about the same variety of fruits and vegetable products which are credited to Georgia. In fact almost every variation of soil, climate or topography in Georgia finds its counterpart in Alabama.

Florida.

This State, not strictly within the Piedmont region, is closely connected with it.

Florida has been called the Italy of America, and it more than justifies the name. Without the historic associations, it has more than the climate and a wider range of fruits. The latitude extends nearer the equator and gives opportunity for many growths which do not flourish in Italy. Even in oranges Florida is supreme, as a hundred and fifty varieties in the Citron fair attested. The crop has already reached several million boxes. There is a long list of fruits and vegetables which thrive in Florida, but aside from oranges the one which is attracting most attention just now is the pineapple. Formerly it was grown almost entirely on islands near Key West, but now it is cultivated extensively on the mainland farther north. Mr. Wm. E. Tabor, of DeSoto county, published in the *Southern States*, a Baltimore magazine, an article from which the following is taken:

"I am of the opinion that this fruit, of which 10,000 can be grown upon an acre and brought to maturity in two years, is far more certain than orange growing, besides being so much more profitable. An expense of $700 will return the amount originally invested in the first and second crops and 50 per cent. additional as profit, while the plantation will then, for at least ten years thereafter, net its owner above all expenses fully $500 per acre. Of course where the pineapple will grow there also will the orange, lemon, lime, pomelo (or grape fruit), mango, guava and other tropical fruits succeed.

"I am on what is called the high sand hills of the lake region, one of the most healthful in the land, where the purest of water is abundant, where there is no malaria as there are no marshy lands or stagnant pools, where even in summer the nights are far pleasanter and cooler than in the North and West.

"In the near vicinity there is land where rice, corn,

sugar-cane, sorghum, potatoes and other farm products can be raised as well as the grasses suited to the South.

"I have visited nearly all the States in the Union, but am convinced that nowhere do the conditions of success exist in greater ratio to the general disadvantages of a country than in Florida.

"In a very few years I shall have a lovely home and a pineapple plantation which will be an annual source of income, and it has not taken over $1,000 to do it. With a less amount even than this it is easy, on account of climate, cheap hands, healthy surroundings, to found a new home in Florida. I shall be pleased to give further information to anyone desiring it."

The *Youth's Companion* prints an article in which the crop of the Keys is estimated at 4,500,000 pineapples, grown on only 700 acres. That paper states that in 1889 a shipload of pineapples sold in England for eleven shillings, or about $2.50 each, and made the grower a small fortune. The chief difficulty is in getting quick transportation for the fruit, but that ought not to be a serious obstacle after the business has grown large enough to make it an object to steamships.

The rapid extension of railroads in Florida has been one of the features of the past decade, and another is the construction of magnificent hotels. The Ponce de Leon at St. Augustine is the finest hotel in America, and the Tampa Bay Hotel is little inferior to it. The Royal Poinciana at Palm Beach is a new favorite, just opened.

As Florida is considered the sanitarium of North America, there is a regular and increasing influx of tourists and health-seekers every winter. It is this that has built up the numerous and costly hotels.

The State has in phosphate deposits a new-found resource which is destined to bring an immense revenue for a long period. Though it has not been five years since the discovery of phosphate rock in Florida, the shipments for manufacture are already immense.

The Carolinas.

The Carolinas come first in order of latitude among the Piedmont States. That portion of their territory which comes properly within the meaning of the term is very similar to the same country extended into the northern parts of Georgia and Alabama. Passing from the hill country of Georgia into South Carolina, the traveler is not sensible of any change unless he turns toward the coast, and even there he finds the counterpart of the coast plain or the middle counties of southern Georgia. There is nearly the same range of latitude, topography, climate and products.

North Carolina differs somewhat from the other Piedmont States. Its topography presents more sharp contrasts, higher mountains, deeper valleys and more picturesque scenery. Still there is near the coast an extension of the Atlantic plain, with the pine belt that runs around the Piedmont region and along the Gulf coast to Texas. North Carolina formerly held supremacy in naval stores, and from that fact its people were called "tar heels," but the reckless cutting and sapping of timber has partly denuded the forests of pine, and Georgia now leads the world in the production of turpentine and rosin. Savannah is the largest market in the world for naval stores.

North Carolina was one of the earliest of the Piedmont States to break away from cotton. It is a singular fact that the negro population is shifting from that State to Mississippi, Arkansas and Texas. It is estimated that within four years nearly a hundred thousand negroes moved from the Carolinas to the Mississippi valley. The heaviest part of this emigration was from North Carolina.

This movement of the colored population was so extensive and so persistent as to attract the attention of scientists and students of sociology, who seem to think that this is the operation of a natural law which carries the negroes from the cooler uplands to the warmer level land of the Mississippi valley.

North Carolina has made a good start in manufactures. Cotton goods are a specialty, both there and in South Carolina, and the mills of these States have in the arduous times of the late depression earned dividends that seem phenomenal even in a period of prosperity. Some of them have declared as much as twenty per cent. on their capital stock. As a result capital, which is skeptical of almost all forms of industry just now, seems to have unbounded confidence in cotton factories, and millions of dollars are going into this branch of industry in the Piedmont States. The investment includes both home capital and heavy additions from New England.

South Carolina has for years held a monopoly of the phosphate industry, and even now leads the world in the production of phosphates for fertilizing purposes. The importance of this may be understood when it is known that the adjoining State of Georgia buys annually 300,000 tons of fertilizers, in which a leading ingredient is acid phosphate. This is the resultant of phosphate rock treated with sulphuric acid. The sulphur used in making the acid formerly came from Sicily, but is now made from iron pyrites. The first of this ore came from Spain, but a fine quality is found in both North Carolina and Georgia, and mines are being opened to supply the fertilizer factories with meterial for making sulphuric acid.

North Carolina has the same general line of minerals as North Georgia, with a very few exceptions. In the quality of her iron ore she surpasses Georgia. The Cranberry mines furnish an ore suitable for making steel.

As in Georgia, the taxation of the Carolinas is moderate and both public and private indebtedness is small. Both States are permeated by the ramifications of the Southern Railway, the great system recently organized of the East Tennessee, the Richmond and Danville and other Southern Railroads.

A new feature of Agriculture in South Carolina is the growing of tea, which has been pronounced a success So far it is not extensive but promises large development. The general features of agriculture in South Carolina are almost identical in scope and character with those of Georgia. In North Carolina there is the important addition of the tobacco industry, which has filled a part of the State with flourishing factories.

In the truck industry the coasts of the Carolinas are especially favored because of their quick connection with Eastern cities by steamer and by the fast schedules of the Atlantic Coast Line Railway system. About Charleston there are extensive fields of strawberries grown for the New York market. The watermelon industry is also an important new feature of agriculture added within the last ten or fifteen years.

Cities of the Piedmont Region.

Atlanta's rapid growth was foretold by the prophetic voice of John C. Calhoun. The late Senator Brown, then a young man, called upon Mr. Calhoun many years before the war, and the conversation turned upon young Brown's future home. "Go to Atlanta," said Mr. Calhoun; "it is the gateway of the South. This is the beginning of a railroad era, and the topography of the country is such that many lines must cross each other at Atlanta. It will be a great center, and there is the place for a young man to make his fortune."

The truth of the prophecy was long ago realized. Atlanta has been known as the Gate City for a quarter of a century, and as she rises to greatness, the words of the old statesman sound like a decree of fate.

There is something remarkable about this city. It is the heart and the inspiration of that progressive spirit which some have been pleased to term "The New South." Ben Hill, the author of that expression, lived here when he breathed upon Georgia the breath of a new life and a new hope; Henry Grady, living here, caught the spirit and the mantle of Hill and kindled anew the fires of industry. His was a genius born for an era—a marvel of inspiration to every faltering industry; the Shakespeare of his day, touching with magic pen wherever his fancy lighted, sweeping the chords of the human heart, and calling into existence new forms of life and beauty. He found rare flowers by the wayside and gleaned from neglected corners of the field more and richer sheaves than Boaz let fall to Ruth.

The kindling flame that leapt from the heart of Grady

never dies on Atlanta's altar, but, climbing higher with each pile of wood and stone, lights the way of progress. Atlanta is the home of a high patriotism, an exalted civic pride, which factions have not weakened and custom has not made commonplace.

It would be tiresome to pile up statistics showing Atlanta's growth. She is all growth—of a recent date. Rising from the flames of war, she began a new existence with four hundred houses, and those shattered and battered by shells. Most of them were wrecks that had to be removed, and scarcely a vestige of the old Atlanta remains. The Atlanta of today is the growth of thirty years—the net result of the work of a generation. Her present business is her growth in business, for she had none thirty years ago; her manufactures are the sum of her industrial progress, for she had no industry thirty years ago; her present population is her growth in population, for she had none thirty years ago. "Go," said Sherman, "for this is war," and they stayed not on the order of their going. The young and the old, the strong and the decrepit, the sick and the women in travail—all went those pitiless days—and fire descended like the wrath of God.

Such was the birth of Atlanta: shattered, beaten and battered, trodden down by alien feet, and christened with a baptism of fire. She was the child of troublous times; the offspring of a revolution; and as Paris was the heart of the great empire which rose out of the reign of terror in France, Atlanta rises, the great heart of the great South, throbbing with the pulsations of a new and greater life.

Atlanta is a cosmopolitan city, with her ten lines of railroad reaching to all quarters of the continent, and her steamship connections and her business connections reaching beyond the sea. The population of 108,000, is mainly of Anglo-Saxon descent, with some admixture of the other races of Europe, but one may meet and converse with people from all parts of the globe—in English, French, German, Spanish, Portuguese, Italian, Arabic and Chinese.

The city has more than a hundred churches and the people are church goers to a noteworthy degree. Education has a firm foundation, not only in the excellent system of public schools, but in the State Institute of Technology, the medical colleges, the various high schools and academies for young men and young women, the schools of art and music, and the libraries with their lecture systems.

The city is compactly built in the central or business portion, but the residence streets, extending far out into the suburbs, well paved and well sewered, furnish the maximum of comfort, light and air, with a minimum of smoke and dust. The electric street car system furnishes quick transit to the suburbs. Over 100 miles of line are in operation and the service is admirable. The streets are lighted by electricity and the buildings by electricity or gas. The price of gas, one dollar per thousand feet, is the lowest in the United States, with one exception. The Grand Opera House is one of the most imposing edifices of the kind in America, and the interior is finished elegantly and decorated with exquisite taste. Two other theaters are open to the public, and Atlanta enjoys attractions that reach few other cities.

The financial institutions and the mercantile element are especially strong here. Atlanta is rapidly becoming a center of capital and industry. The manufacturing element has strength in diversity. Mr. Grady often said that Atlanta bore to Birmingham or Chattanooga the relation which Philadelphia, with its varied industries, bore to the iron city of Pittsburgh. The city of brotherly love had its strength and its uniform prosperity in the multitude and the diversity of its industries, and so has Atlanta.

Atlanta also resembles Philadelphia in the number of home owners. The proportion of rented houses is lower here than in most cities, and the proportion of home owners larger. Atlanta is the home of building and loan associations, both local and national, and these institutions have been phenomenally successful.

The press of Atlanta is especially strong. The *Constitution* has long maintained its place at the head of Southern dailies, and the *Journal* has set a new pattern for the afternoon press.

Architecture in Atlanta bids fair to surpass that of any other Southern city. The State Capitol, costing a million dollars, is a model of classic style, imposing in proportions and magnificent in detail. The Equitable Building, the Grand Opera House, the Inman Building, the Silvey Building, the Kimball House and the Aragon Hotel, are some of the chief structures.

AUGUSTA.

Augusta is a fine old city, with historic associations reaching back a hundred years. For generations it has been the home of wealth and culture, and has also been a seat of industry, especially in the manufacture of cotton. It is one of the largest inland markets for cotton and a great mill town. The census for 1890 shows that during the previous decade Augusta made a greater percentage gain in manufacturing than any other Southern city, reckoning by the increase of capital, employes and wages.

Augusta is the headquarters of the Georgia Railroad and Banking Company, whose line, though fifty years old, owes no bonded debt and has never killed a passenger—a record not equaled by any other railroad in the United States.

The *Chronicle*, the leading daily newspaper, has a national reputation, and its editor, Hon. Patrick Walsh, has just completed a term in the United States Senate.

SAVANNAH.

Savannah is the oldest city in Georgia, dating from the time of Oglethorpe. It is a solid, thoroughgoing city, with less of bustle and activity than Atlanta, but able and sagacious in trade. This statement is borne out by the fact that Savannah takes toll on practically the whole of Georgia's export products. She receives about as many bales of cotton as the State raises, and in naval stores she enjoys almost a monopoly. In lumber she has to divide with Brunswick and Darien, but takes the bulk of the trade. It is no wonder that her docks and wharves are immense and that a great railway system has been built up from that point. In the commercial expansion for which the Southern States are preparing, Savannah must have a large part, and her future must unquestionably be a great one.

BIRMINGHAM.

Birmingham is the center of a region on which the eyes of the world are turned, without parallel in the close proximity of massive deposits of iron, coal and limestone. It is an iron city, and its history is the history of the iron market to a great extent. Thirty large furnaces, with many related industries of the iron family, have been built up there. The plants were constructed on the best pattern, and when Andrew Carnegie visited Birmingham he said that Alabama had profited by the experience of Pennsylvania, and her machinery was superior to that of many establishments in Pennsylvania and Ohio. The Southern iron masters developed remarkable strength in competition with Pennsylvania for the production of iron at low prices, but even the advantage of superior economy in the Birmingham region did not prevent the prolonged depression from having its effect upon the iron city. With reaction in the iron market Birmingham will undoubtedly renew her vigor, and a great growth is in store for the region. The industries are of immense proportions, and once fully in motion again, will employ an immense amount of labor and produce a great wage fund.

Birmingham suffered severely a few years ago from the speculative fever which ran through the Piedmont region, visiting especially the iron towns. The price of real estate doubled, redoubled and quadrupled in a short time, and the people became intoxicated by the suddenness with which fortunes were made. Everyone seemed to be making and for a time all went wildly. Then came the inevitable collapse and the slow, painful shrinkage of years. Most of the iron towns went through a similar experience, but Birmingham was hard hit. The place had great wealth, and long bore up well under the strain. The shrinkage process is over and the time cannot be far distant when a healthy revival of industry in the Birmingham district will set in.

The Cotton States and International Exposition.

A NEW ERA WILL BE INAUGURATED WITH THE OPENING OF THIS GREAT FAIR AT ATLANTA ON THE 18TH OF SEPTEMBER, 1895.

For the first time in their history, the Cotton States have attempted an Exposition of truly international character. The fact that few of the Southern States were represented at the World's Fair of 1893 led to the projection of this enterprise; and since its inception, other causes have combined to expand it to proportions far greater than those originally contemplated. This Exposition was organized when trade was depressed, industry was partially paralyzed, and manufactures were seeking some outlet for surplus products. The home market was weak, and the natural course was to look abroad for an increase of demand. So it became one of the principal objects of the projectors of the Cotton States and International Exposition to promote closer trade relations and larger commerce between the United States and the countries of South and Central America. The field of operation was extended to take in all countries of commercial importance ; and Europe will be largely represented and largely interested in this display. A collection of the resources of the Southern States superior to any heretofore made will be brought together, and in this work the important services of the United States Geological Survey, the Bureau of Forestry, the Fish Commission and the Department of Agriculture have been enlisted. In addition, all branches of the Government work will be represented by exhibits. The United States Government has endorsed the Exposition by an appropriation of $200,000 for an exhibit, and the Government building will be one of the largest on the grounds. The commissioners appointed to represent the different branches of service in this work have entered actively upon it, and the indications are that the exhibit, though not covering so large a space as at Chicago, will be fully as interesting, if not more so, because of improvements suggested by that experience.

There will be exhibits from a number of South American countries. The Argentine Republic has voted $25,000 in gold for an exhibit, Venezuela, Honduras and Nicaragua have sent formal acceptances of an invitation to take part, and President Diaz has said that Mexico would be represented. Exhibits will be made by important industries in England, Germany, Austria, Hungary, Italy, France and

Belgium, and commissioners have been sent to those countries to arrange with exhibitors.

A fine array of State and Railroad exhibits will be made, and these, with the foreign exhibits, will fill a number of handsome structures to be erected on the grounds.

Great care has been exercised in dealing with exhibits to encourage those illustrating, by actual operations, the best and latest methods of art and industry. It is sought in this way to heighten the educational value of the Exposition, and to exclude mere merchandise or cumbersome material.

This Exposition is expected to give a tremendous impulse to trade between these States and South America, and this effect will be increased by the opening of the Nicaragua Canal, to which both the great political parties are committed. In the same way trade between the Southern ports and Europe will be increased. Atlanta is known abroad as never before, and because of this Exposition the Southern States are attracting world-wide attention.

Southern Immigration and Improvement Co.

JAMES P. DAY,	J. H. MOUNTAIN,	J. MARK BISHOP,
President.	Manager.	Sec. & Treas.

45 NORTH BROAD ST., ATLANTA, GA.

www.ingramcontent.com/pod-product-compliance
Lightning Source LLC
Chambersburg PA
CBHW030907170426
43193CB00009BA/768